Healing Trauma from the Inside Out

Practices from the East and West

PAMELA TINKHAM, MSW, LCSW

with Linda Mortenson

Copy Editor and Assistance
Karin Gerber (TheWebsiteApproach.com)
Editor
Linda Mortenson
Artwork
Sarah Szabo
Book Design
Barbara Aronica-Buck (bookdesigner.com)

ISBN: 1543049923 (Paperback)
ISBN-13: 978-1543049923 (Paperback)

This book is dedicated to my family,
friends, clients . . . and my angels in heaven.

Contents

Acknowledgments

It is a gift to be able to publish a book. It has been a dream of mine. I have many people to thank who have been involved in the process over the past ten years.

First and foremost I would like to thank Linda Mortenson, my superb editor. I could not have completed this project without your support and intelligence. You are a true friend and our friendship continues to grow. Thank you for all the fun times we have had, acting like high school kids!

I would like to say a special thank you to my family for their love and support. Thank you to my husband, Chris. I love you so much and appreciate all that you do! You accepted me working in the middle of the night on the book and I am truly grateful for your love and support. Thanks to Whiskey and Red, my kitties, who give me unconditional love and nurturing on a daily basis and to Whiskey who acts as my therapy cat and adds his expertise to some of my sessions. Snowflake and Salina, in heaven, have shined their love and light on me eternally. My Dad, Irwin Gerber, for his love, tenderness and kind heart. My Mom, Joyce Gerber, and her partner, Bobby Robinson, for their generosity of spirit. Thank you to my brother, Jon Gerber, who teaches me on a daily basis how to thrive in the midst of challenges and to my sister, Nadine Benoit, and brother-in-law, Kevin Benoit, for their continued support over the years. Gratitude to my nieces and nephew, Allison, Jacqueline, and Eric Benoit, whom I love so much! May you continue to see the world through innocent eyes! Love to my nieces, Erica and Jessica Robinson, and sister-in-law, Karen Robinson, and Mom Tinkham, 91 years old and sharp as a whip. Thanks to my extended family in Long Island, NY, Canada and Israel. Bradley Carbone, you continue to teach me lessons of gratitude and appreciation for life.

Professionally there are many advisors and mentors to thank. To begin with thank you to Sally Eberhardt, MA, NCPsyA, for your time and support consulting for the book. Karin Gerber, my copy editor, website designer and assistant, you are brilliant. A special thank you to Rev. Dr. Nadja Fidelia for writing the foreword and for being my dearest long-term friend and spiritual advisor and to Angel Lau for being our Angel for now and always. Yasmin Namini, thank you for your friendship, support and empowerment! My mentor and guest writer, Dave Asomaning, PhD, thank you for being my God connection; and thank you to Cantor Magda Fishman for your beautiful and soulful contribution to the *Surrender* chapter. Randall D. Martin, PhD, thank you for your motivational and intelligent contribution about the importance of fitness and mental health.

Thank you to Elizabeth DiRusso and Alexis Brooks for your guidance with the publishing process. Thank you to Barbara Aronica-Buck, my book designer, overseer and guardian angel for the book. My artist and guest writer,

Sarah Szabo, your artwork shows the beauty of life and hope for new possibilities. My designers for business materials, Paul and Ellen Golden, you have made it possible for me to shine and thank you to Patrick and Susan Kelly for your immense support over the years. Thank you to Beth Huisking for your technical support for my presentations and to Margie Fusco, Jon Gerber, Liz Ross, Daniel Rosenstein, Susan Holzman, and Joyce Gerber for your assistance with final steps before publishing. And thank you, Liz, for your expert proofreading!

Dr. Nazanine Khairkah, thank you for believing in my holistic practice and trusting me with your patients over the past ten years! Dr. Mark Banschick, thank you for your friendship, for helping me to be published and thank you to your son, Gabriel, for introducing us! Dr. Bruce Shapiro, thank you for your expertise and for being available to my clients. Dr. Richard Strongwater and Dr. Chetan Vaid, you were the first medical doctors to believe in my holistic model. Gratitude to Caryn Marcus, Lisa Colvin, LPC, Heather Edwards, LMHC, Kathryn Crosby, LCSW, and Brad Gilden, DPT, for your continued support and inspiration over the years. And a very special shout out to my two professors from Fordham University who inspired me to write this book, Dr. Robert Youdin and Dr. Rosa Perez-Koenig.

Thank you to the entire Temple Beth El community in Stamford, Connecticut, The Somatic Experiencing® Trauma Institute SE™ community, and our entire ski community. Thank you to my current and past yoga teachers, and to my teaching partners, Monica Keady and Ilene

Friedman. Blessings and gratitude to my Reiki Masters and energy workers, Theresa Joseph, Linda Fallo-Mitchell, Beth Leas, Connie Jones, Gene Krachehl, James Murray and Ldwain.

Lastly, thank you to my yogis, peers, clients, and friends. It is because of you that I get to live my life's purpose each and every day. I am sure I have forgotten someone so here's a big thanks to you as well!

With gratitude,
Pamela

Foreword

"When God made Pam, He took extra special care." Pamela helped me become a much stronger person from within over the course of twenty-five years. When she asked me to write the foreword for her book I was honored and gladly accepted as our love and appreciation for each other was mutual. Learning to manage my physical, mental, and spiritual well-being has been my top priority. I was a single mother who juggled various roles such as an investment banker and trader on Wall Street, a director of multiple non-profit boards, and a licensed Reverend.

While working as a trader at a top investment banking firm, I experienced a tremendous amount of anxiety and stress daily. In addition to trading securities, my language skills led me to the coverage of international clients which involved frequent travel. My work responsibilities took a toll on my health. When my doctor put me on the medication, Tenormin, after being diagnosed with a heart condition, I realized that something had to give. As I was not about to give up my job as an emerging markets trader, a job which I enjoyed immensely, I decided that I needed to make time to take better care of my body. This revelation led me to Pamela.

Back in 1992, she was a highly sought after personal trainer. I purchased a 10-session package from a trading floor colleague who was working with Pamela, but could

not fulfill her training commitment due to a hectic schedule. That was the best purchase of my life, as it was the
first step in the right direction to balance my life; also, I
met Pamela, an amazing human being who focused on a
holistic approach to well-being by caring for mind, body
and soul. To this day, Pamela continues to be a very close
friend, confidant and spiritual counsel.

Pamela has always been humble, kind, dedicated
and passionate in her efforts. She is continually trying to
maximize her contribution to society. For example, we
adopted an elementary school in downtown New York
City as a community project. Pamela shopped and packed
holiday gifts for 250 students and taught them to sing and
dance as part of a holiday performance for their parents.
I will never forget the pride on the children's faces as they
received such attention and encouragement.

Pamela's kindness not only extends to people but
also to animals. Despite being devastated by the traumatic events on September 11, she worked diligently with
the ASPCA and rescued my cat, Paisley, who was stuck in
my apartment in Battery Park City, across the street from
the fallen towers. She convinced a military person to
accompany her into my dark apartment and called out to
Paisley until he came to her. She saved Paisley's life with
her courage and selfless act.

After witnessing the pain and trauma of September
11, Pamela set off to obtain a Master's Degree in Social
Work to extend her breadth and depth of therapeutic
techniques to help those in need of physical, mental and
emotional healing. She graduated at the top of her class at

Fordham. Along the way, she inspired me to continue my own ten-year quest for a Doctorate in Ministry at the New York Theological Seminary.

Pamela continues to be a partner in my own journey for wholeness and wellness. She was my Reiki Master's program leader and certified me as a Reiki Master. She encouraged me to do yoga (Bikram, Vinyasa) and meditation as part of my overall routine. She introduced me to the synagogue and her own spiritual practice which is embedded in her discipline of giving from the heart. She has been a great supporter of my startup organization, Women's Anointed Mission (WAM) that I host in New York City; and she still works side-by-side as I build a venue for successful women in the financial and non-profit fields to cross-network and share personal stories of spiritual liberation.

As a minister, my ability to love scripture for its figurative qualities allows me to find God in places beyond the confines of holy text and in people in all corners of the world. My own journey to learn about other faiths has evolved over time and has deepened my knowledge of people, cultures, and scripture. When I first attended a Hindu temple, I was amazed that after practicing Siddha Yoga for over six years, I had never fully appreciated the Hindu worship behind my meditation practices, such as the recital of the Guru Gita daily. I have learned that being open to my ignorance and to new experiences gives me a fuller understanding of the spirit within me. Many people around the world are like me, and they follow the meditation and spiritual practices of the Hindu tradition despite the fact that they are not observant Hindus. What is the meaning of that interconnectedness in a multi-faith setting, and how can we learn and duplicate this phenomenon? This is where dialogue becomes essential to facilitate sharing of cultures and traditions and to help people of different backgrounds find a space of connection.

In my own search for identity and a sense of belonging, and a need to depend on a force greater than myself, I have come to see praying as a practice of digging within for strength. Praying allows me to discern life's true meaning and my role in it. Praying provides dedicated times of reflection, worship, unity and community love when done with others. Through prayer, we find our story, our path, our understanding for our purpose in life. Whether God is essence, oneness, supreme reality, or formless Divine, all religions and faiths need prayer to put its beliefs in practice. This demonstration of holiness and sacredness via a worship activity such as prayer, meditation, chanting, or other forms of dialogue with God, allows us to commune with God, a religious deity, or one's own soul.

Whether we are operating from a calling from God, or simply from our heart, underneath our genuine urge to foster change, to heal and contribute to our society, lurk the demons from our own childhood. Self-healing is a vital step for living a healthy and purposeful life. We need to heal ourselves before trying to help others in our community.

This is what Pamela's book is trying to do. All change involves loss, but everything we lose makes room for growth and transformation. It creates space for new divine partnerships that are critical to our destiny. There will be all manners of change to face in our lifetimes: changes that will redirect, rejuvenate, relocate, or reposition us. We will also face changes that will stun, shake, and break us; these are changes that will stop us in our tracks, as well as changes that will liberate us. Regardless, we must be willing to pay the price of change.

By harnessing our God-given gift to be of use to face worldly challenges, we extend the legacy of great leaders, women and men, from all walks of life. By surrendering to our inner light, we garner strength and courage to speak truth to power, push back on dogma and manmade rules, demand our rights and take actions that can transform a society for all our good. The culmination of my life testimony, my corporate career, my seminary studies, and my experiences as a woman minister, are my commitment to answering God's call.

Our communities need healing and acceptance to really become global, inclusive, non-sexist and non-racist. We need an awakening and an enlightenment experience that reconnects us to our inner light so we can tap into our gifts and talent confidently, without human-made blockages and internal resistance to success.

My entire life thus far has been dedicated to creating a more fair society by living in service to my family and my community. I do not live a day without shepherding another human being. When I reflect on my daily activities, I see myself move through a myriad of roles: mentor, teacher, advocate, and healer.

Pamela and I both share these leadership roles and we support each other in living our passion. I cannot attain my achievements without a coach and a natural born healer by my side. Pamela has been that anchor for me, and I continue to lean on her understanding and insights as guidance in my purposeful life.

Pamela and I have much in common. We are self-made, self-starters and highly motivated. Pamela will continue to bring a strong voice for the future of healing with all of her training and experience. She incorporates her zeal for innovative ideas into her role as a therapist. Her path throughout her career leads up to this next accomplishment in her book. She is incredibly generous in writing this book to prepare many to start their journey of healing consciously and intentionally. This is an incredible gift and much needed in our society, which is so filled with distractions and unrealistic expectations that take us away from taking care of the Self.

It has been a delight for me to watch Pamela's career evolve; I witnessed her transformation from a personal trainer to a therapist and a leader in the field of healing. I am not surprised that today she wants to complement all of her expertise with this book to increase her contributions to the community at large. She will not just continue to be successful in whatever she pursues; she will always be significant as she will impact our health, well-being and happiness.

—The Reverend Dr. Nadja Fidelia

Introduction

Healing Trauma from the Inside Out, Practices from the East and West came about from my own personal traumas and the ability to learn from my history and take that knowledge into the psychotherapy room to help others with their traumas. My intention is to reach as many people as possible with this book, a practical "how to" guide, so that healing trauma can be easier and more peaceful for others. The book is not to be misunderstood as any type of medical treatment, nor will it work for everyone. It is geared towards the individual soul seeker and inquirer of inner knowledge of the body-mind connection. Also, trauma can range from having an emotional upset to having major abuse, a physical accident, a surgery or any other upsetting event. Traumas are stored in the body and may not be remembered in the mind until attention and awareness are brought to them with the intention of healing. Anything that compromises your nervous system can be considered trauma.

I began this "East to West" journey in 2002 while attending Fordham University for my Master's in Social Work. I had an advisor, Dr. Rosa Perez-Koenig, who became an important figure in my learning. She was a feisty, sassy, New York City lady with a great sense of humor and a heart of gold. Dr. Koenig made a lasting impression on me and on my work as a therapist. The first day of class she entered and said right at the beginning of class, "Do any of you have a problem with me because I'm Latino? I am asking because you may have a judgment about my accent or my nationality." She went on to explain that we all have judgments, and the best thing to do is to speak about them in order to reveal the "elephant in the room" so that the air is clear for the therapeutic work to begin. I appreciated her because of her wit, honesty, humor and the comfort she had in her own skin. When I learned that she would be my advisor through my graduate studies, I was truly happy.

One day while in her office for an advisory session, Dr. Koenig suggested some publications to read, including her own book called *Social Work in the Era of Devolution*. Another book she recommended was called *Psychotherapy East and West, a Unifying Paradigm*. Dr. Koenig thought it would resonate with me because of my background in fitness and yoga. I never imagined before that point that I could be a "Yoga-Psychotherapist," incorporating Eastern philosophy into my evidence-based Western psychotherapy practice. In looking back on this scenario from fifteen years ago, it is almost like she knew what my path would be before I did. Thank you, Rosa!

Another outstanding professor at Fordham University who inspired me in many ways was Dr. Robert Youdin. He is a published author, scholar and researcher and continues to have a lasting impression on me even though I have only spoken to him once in the past 10 years. My final clinical paper for his class, *Clinical Theory and Practice,* asked for knowledge of three psychological theories. My passion was so intense that I also wrote about a fourth theory, *Psychotherapy and Yoga*. Dr. Youdin's comments at the end of my paper were extremely positive. I held onto his encouraging words to continue my path and create my own individualistic combination of psychotherapy and yoga.

My Fordham professors, amongst earlier mentors, were instrumental in my growth and success. I think they sensed something within me even before I was aware of it. In my younger years, I did not believe in myself and felt a discomfort within my being. Often when clients enter my practice, they have this same discomfort in their skin. I was not fully embodied back then, and I did not have a recipe of how to obtain confidence, self-esteem and inner awareness. My hope as you are reading this book is that you find an easy way to connect to your true self and your essence in order to heal from the demons or wounds within. It's never easy to face the parts of ourselves that we do not like and disconnect from. If we learn to tolerate these areas in small increments, over time our tolerance for these areas becomes greater and our need to suppress them becomes less. Instead of impulse behaviors or outbursts to our family, friends and loved ones, we will be able to soften and integrate those fully charged areas of ourselves in a way that they do not lash out and overtake our being. More will be explored throughout the book on how trauma can manifest in physical, mental and emotional symptoms and how we may use unhealthy vices in order to avoid our inner selves and our deepest wounds.

The **Psycho-tips** at the end of each chapter will provide a brief summary of where to begin. The term "psycho-tips" is intended in good faith and humor. My hope as you read this book is that you approach it with an open heart and mind. Not everything will resonate with you. I request that you discard what does not feel right for you and embrace what does. Thank you for reading ahead!

> With love and gratitude,
> Pamela

Part One

From Trauma
to Hope

1

From 9/11 to Therapy

"No snowflake ever falls in the wrong place."
–Zen Proverb

Seeking to help others with their traumas began when I was five years old, believe it or not! I was the kid on the block who would befriend someone no one played with. I had compassion and empathy, even at such a young age. I went through a selfish period from my teens through my early thirties; and it was not until I was a block away from the World Trade Center on 9/11/01 running for my life, that I had a complete transformation.

This event for me actually had a silver lining and brought me to where I am today. As I sat with strangers in the shelter of a car with debris from the fallen towers raining all around us, I asked God to let me live that day. I promised I would do something more meaningful with my life and pursue a career where I could work with people in need. I would gain the confidence to get a Master's Degree in Social Work so that I could pursue a career as a psychotherapist.

Needless to say, here I am! I needed that confidence, although it was not always easy to come by. Up to this point my focus had been on being a dancer, performer, and personal fitness trainer. Keeping fit, in shape, and looking good were a requirement in this field and a preoccupation of mine in my youth. My sister, on the other hand, had always been more focused on her studies and was a straight A student. My teachers would say to me, "Why can't you be more like your sister?"

Truthfully, I did not want to be more like my sister because I was having too much fun dancing and singing, especially working on cruise ships after getting my B.A. in Dance. I will never forget those days of sun tanning, signing autographs and thinking I was famous and fabulous. It was all about me.

After 9/11 that all changed. I am happy to say that I found the true self I was supposed to be all along. I found my loving compassion for humanity and I discovered my true purpose in life. I started the new journey first as a social worker in various hospitals and clinics, then as a psychotherapist with a fitness element, and later added yoga, mindfulness and meditation to my psychotherapy practice and Reiki to my yoga classes. Currently I am trained as a somatic therapist (therapy within the body) and will be certified as a Somatic Experiencing Practitioner (SEP) from The Somatic Experiencing® Trauma Institute SE™, created by the world renowned Peter Levine. While fitness, yoga, mindfulness, meditation and Reiki are all tools at my disposal, I have found my true passion in life is helping clients heal from trauma.

The experience I lived through on 9/11 led me to this place and gave me the empathy and deep understanding of pure human suffering. I am very lucky.

So many did not make it out alive that day. God bless their souls and may they all be our angels in heaven resting in peace.

Amen

Psycho-tips

- Sometimes our deepest traumas can be our greatest openings if we are lucky enough to have lived through them.
- Trauma may connect you to your purpose in life.
- Trauma may lead you to a cause greater than yourself, for the greater good.
- Recognize if your life is self-focused or focused on the well-being of others.
- Confidence is an inside job—we must find it from within instead of superficially.
- Empathy is a gift—use it with all that you do.
- There is a silver lining within the deepest traumas, even if you cannot see it for years to come.

2

Healing Trauma Begins
With the Body First

*"Looking inside ourselves can be the most terrify-
ing thing we can do. Yet we can exhaust ourselves looking everywhere else. The truth we
glimpse when we look within connects us to the
world. We begin to see our purpose here is to
provide, care for and be available to the world."*
—Vincent Dopulos, LMHC, LPC, RDT

My work as a therapist initially began with treatment
focused primarily on the mind, not the body. I used Cognitive Behavioral Therapy (CBT), along with a strengths
perspective (focusing on people's strengths rather than
problems) and physical fitness model, to treat and coach
individuals with eating disorders at a physician's office in
Westchester, NY. I loved the CBT approach at the time; it
made sense to me because it is evidence-based and
seemed intuitive. In fact, without even being aware of it,
I had been practicing CBT on myself for years. I could easily recognize a negative thought pattern and the associated feelings and emotions that came along with it. CBT
has a huge place in the field of mental health and there

is ample research on its benefits. However, for me, working only on the "head" and not also incorporating the body seemed doomed to fail. In my own therapy and self-examination, I could see that the mind could not be healed without a coinciding focus on the body.

I recently had a young client's father tell me how helpful the work I did with the body-mind connection was for his daughter during a time where she was in great distress. He specifically said that it was the combination of CBT and physical fitness that helped his daughter.

Irvin Yalom, one of the first theorists of group therapy, stated that "It is the relationship that heals." There is something to be said for loosening the boundaries between the clinical therapy room and the gym floor! My young client got better because I was both a therapist and a physical trainer. The training piece of it allowed her to explore her physical strengths and abilities and connect to her body rather than simply be locked in her thoughts. Hence, my work that began as an experiential exploration in 2002, has blossomed into a well-regarded and effective treatment for a variety of mental health concerns including anxiety, depression, eating disorders, bi-polar disorder, borderline personality disorder, addictions, relationship issues and traumatic events.

The CBT world is now presenting more research on a body-centered approach. There is a wonderful, in-depth psychology book called *The Handbook of Body Psychotherapy & Somatic Psychology* by Marlock, Weiss, Young and Soth, that explores each theory and provides the most current research on the interconnectedness between the body and mind. This nearly 1,000 page hard-cover book keeps me interested for hours at a time and has been a great resource in furthering my knowledge on this topic. This "handbook" is only a fraction of the work being done on this front around the world.

In conclusion, I am convinced after many years of training and personal experience that you must begin by healing the body first, and the mind will follow. Along with many of my peers in the field of psychotherapy, I initially had it backwards. I now know that to heal from trauma you must first start with the body, face the demons within, calm the mind and be in the present moment.

Psycho-tips

- Trauma is stored in the body, and this affects the mind and the spirit.
- Healing from trauma is best supported by somatic (body-oriented) therapies. Work on the body first and the "head" will follow.
- Physical health affects mental health which affects spiritual well-being.
- Cognitive Behavioral Therapy (CBT) is an evidence-based approach to healing that is now presenting more research on the integration of body-oriented therapies for healing trauma.
- The therapeutic bond and relationship between the client and therapist can be exceptionally healing. "It is the relationship that heals."
- Healing trauma takes time, patience and an interconnected approach.
- Facing the demons in the body, calming the mind and being completely present are the first steps towards *Healing Trauma from the Inside Out*.

Facing Your Fear
and Owning Your Power

"Don't ask what the world needs. Ask what makes you come alive and go do it. Because what the world needs are people who have come alive."

–Howard Thurman

When a publisher recently reached out and suggested I write a book, I contacted her immediately. I had started a book about ten years ago but had never finished it. Now with the push of this publisher my excitement about writing was renewed. I still had the negative voice in my head periodically telling me that I could not possibly write a book. However, my confidence and courage through years of my own personal reflection and from successfully treating others in my private practice took over and I started to write. Overcoming fear can feel impossible. As I look back on those fearful thoughts I realize how debilitating they can be. I hope as you read through the book, you will feel inspired to overcome your fearful thoughts as well. They are just thoughts, and thoughts are very often not based on reality.

Why is it so difficult for some of us to be powerful?

Why do we fear success even more than we fear failure? Why is it so easy to praise and idealize others as if they are more special than we are? We are all unique and special. We all have a God-given purpose in life. Once we step into that purpose and own that power, we can allow our beautiful light to shine. My dear friend Nadja, who wrote the foreword for this book, states that certain people are "light dimmers," and they can challenge us along the way. In this book, I will encourage you to conquer and embrace those challenges and move forward with confidence, grace, purpose and acceptance in the most genuine way you can. I am grateful to be able to assist clients in facing their fears and owning their power.

Owning our power is about accepting ourselves for better or worse. It is also about having a relationship with those parts of ourselves that we would like to put away forever and noticing with present awareness that we can touch on those areas without becoming attached to them. It is like the monster we want to kill. Many times we want to separate off or destroy a disappointing part of ourselves. As we do this, our psyches react and fight back even stronger. Accordingly, the more we deny our emotions and disappointing parts of ourselves, the stronger they come back to fight with a vengeance. We can try to live our lives splitting off parts of ourselves. However, this coping only works for a short while. As soon as there is a crisis or life gets unmanageable, the parts that we cut off will shut us down and paralyze us. Until we accept and love all parts of ourselves, we cannot move forward successfully in life. It was not until I was in my thirties that I fully became able to love myself both inside and out. It took time, practice, and dedication to do the work that was required to grow and learn. Luckily, there were plenty of mentors along the way who led me in the right direction. I am fortunate to have all the people I have in my life and, I am truly grateful. Also, I believe the reason I can truly relate to my clients is because I "get" them. I have an innate ability to support people through their life challenges. I assist them in noticing their obstacles to success and support them in remaining confident and empowered so that they are not overwhelmed by the fear of these obstacles.

Let us explore how we can become calm within the storms that life throws our way. The first thing we must do is recognize when we are consumed by fear and know that we cannot accomplish anything if we are in that state. Once we recognize our fear, there are many options. One option is to simply write about it. Putting the words down on paper can diminish the ferocity and intensity of the fear. Another option is to engage in physical activity. The physical activity will cause the anxiety to dissipate as it moves through the body. The final option available is to drop into your body. You can do this through mindfulness, meditation, yoga, or simply feeling your feet on the ground. You may also do a body scan to notice where the anxiety lies. A simple body scan can be done with your eyes open or closed. (Open eyes can help in a fearful state.) A body scan brings your attention and awareness to each body part.

An important figure in mindfulness is John Kabat-Zinn, PhD. He is one of the main pioneers responsible for bringing the Eastern practice of mindfulness and meditation to the medical community in the Western part of the world. His contribution has helped make mindfulness widely practiced and respected in America. Kabat-Zinn states to "Stop and drop into your body," which is a simple but valuable technique. Sometimes this is a scary place, but this practice will assist you in being able to keep your personal power. Beginning to tolerate the sensations in the body is what somatic therapy is all about. We start small and slow and then grow to be able to tolerate unpleasant emotions and sensations that are held within the body. This way we can begin to accept and release the emotions.

As you move forward with the chapters in the book, we will practice mindfulness, meditation and visualization exercises to help you cope with and eventually heal your traumas, become grounded, and own your personal power. My intention is to share what I have learned over the years of therapy and practice and to inspire you. I am your equal partner in life's journey to wellness.

Psycho-tips

- Become aware of the fear that is paralyzing you so that you can work on owning your power.
- Decide whether you want to explore the fear by breathing into it and noticing bodily sensations, or would prefer to go outside for a walk or a run.
- Do what feels organic and best for you when facing your fears.
- If you decide to check in with your bodily sensations and perform a body scan you may keep your eyes open or closed as you "Stop and drop into the body."
- Breathe into the areas of fear to help dissipate them.
- Accept and love yourself even if you do not feel it organically in the present moment.
- Write down your fears or share them with someone you love and trust.

4

Living with Depression

"Loneliness is underestimating your right to thrive and your ability to receive fellowship with others."

—Ldwain

Living with depression can be incredibly debilitating. Clinical depression can stop you in your tracks for no apparent reason. Sometimes a chemical imbalance is to blame; other times poor circumstances bring it on, and this can be equally paralyzing.

In my experience, even the most serious depression cases had successful improvement through a combination of psychotherapy, health, fitness, yoga, medication, and, in many cases, spirituality. In addition, mindfulness and meditation play a huge role in helping people cope with depression.

Clients usually describe their depression as a huge black hole in the center of their being that seems to permeate downward in a spiraling vortex and sucks the life out of them. They also describe the feeling of emptiness, hopelessness and wanting to die even if they are not having suicidal thoughts. The feeling of not wanting to be here on this planet underscores the enormity of their suffering. I am eternally grateful that none of my clients have gone over that edge. There have been close calls, and I am thankful to have had the opportunity to intervene in people's deepest moments of despair to offer some form of hope and safety.

As you read forward you will see many suggestions for coping with depression, anxiety, Post-Traumatic Stress Disorder (PTSD) and arguments pro and con for treating with medication versus treating with fitness, yoga, and other natural modalities. I am a strong believer in medication if you are having suicidal thoughts, feelings or tendencies. Many clients come in with severe depression and do not want to go on medication. If someone comes to me with an overwhelming depression and wants to try psychotherapy first and avoid medication, I still encourage them to go for a psychiatric evaluation. Just having the medication in their medicine cabinet can provide some relief from symptoms.

Many times when people are depressed they find some immediate relief just from making an appointment with a therapist and taking the first step in asking for help. This is a huge accomplishment in treating depression. There is no shame in taking care of yourself. It is an act of courage and bravery to go to therapy. In later chapters I will offer you numerous coping skills as you embark on your journey. Even if you only take away one skill that works for you, my intention for this book will be accomplished.

Psycho-tips

- Depression is an illness that needs to be treated.
- Depression can immobilize you if you do not get help.
- Calling for help is the first step in alleviating some of the severity of the depression.
- Clinical depression often needs to be medicated in conjunction with psychotherapy and a fitness regimen.
- Yoga, meditation, mindfulness and exercise can help to alleviate the symptoms and severity of the depression.
- If you are having any suicidal thoughts, a psychiatric evaluation is necessary and indicated.
- If you take away at least one coping skill from this book that helps you with your depression, my intention will have been met.

5

Living with Anxiety

"Living with anxiety is like having every day feel like you're going on a job interview or awaiting test results. The myriad of thoughts and worry never ends."
                                                —Jon Gerber

Anxiety is tricky because often people like the motivation that comes from their anxiety. In Rollo May's book entitled *The Meaning of Anxiety,* the author speaks about the positive aspects of living with anxiety. People who are anxious may actually get a lot of work done in a short amount of time because it helps them alleviate the extra stress that procrastination can cause.

Another thing I have noticed in the years of practicing is that people who enter treatment with anxiety often do not see or understand that they have anxiety. They usually come in with stress and feel fearful about next steps. The anxiety is often ego-syntonic (viewed as acceptable with one's personality and beliefs) which means that it is so much a part of their schema (a pattern of thought or behavior) that it does not bother them. It is often unrecognized until a friend or partner provides feedback to them about their anxieties. At this point they still may not want to address the anxiety, especially if it has served them well in business and in getting things accomplished in life.

If your anxiety is working for you as a motivator, by all means use it to achieve your goals. However, there is a price to pay for this if it becomes constant, obsessive or compulsive. The body and the nervous system need to rest and relax. The nervous system is on high alert (sympathetic nervous system) when you have a deadline to meet and is relaxed when you do meditation or yoga and tap into your para-sympathetic nervous system. Both are needed and balance is warranted when you are working in overdrive. Pranayama (pra-na-ya-ma) in yoga, the regulation of the breath through certain exercises and techniques, will assist you in calming down the nervous system so that your motivation does not turn into a mental and physical disorder.

An easy way to determine if you are taxing the nervous system while you are in a motivated state is to see if there is any tension in your jaw, head, neck, shoulders, lower back or buttocks. Checking in with your body will surely allow your mind to notice if the anxiety is becoming dangerous for your entire system. "Dangerous" may seem too extreme of a word; but over time, if you do not rest and relax your body it will break down, and illness can occur. It sounds simple to just take care of yourself, but so many of us fall short in this area.

Many clients have told me they would much rather have anxiety than depression. How about not having either? That would be the best outcome in order for you to thrive!

Psycho-tips

- Notice if you have anxiety, and do not dismiss people's feedback if they tell you that you do.
- Notice when your system is in overdrive.
- Use your anxiety as a motivator.
- Start to recognize when your motivating anxiety turns into an obsession or compulsion.
- Check in with your body to see if you are holding tension in the jaw, head, neck, shoulders, lower back or buttocks.
- Be sure to rest and relax.
- You can use yoga, pranayama (yoga breathing) or meditation to tap into the para-sympathetic nervous system in order to restore emotional and physical equilibrium.

6

A Word From the Artist

by Sarah Szabo

"An expression of our inner experience through art creates wisdom."

–Heather Edwards, LMHC

Before we go any further, I would like to introduce the artist for the book, Sarah Szabo. Sarah speaks about fear and hope and how the connection of body and mind was initially introduced to her through my practice years ago. I met her when she was a young teenager and I am humbled and honored to have her as part of this amazing project:

"I am the artist who painted the cover for the book as well as the artwork inside. The cover is a white and purple orchid, lounging on a plate of pearly river rocks with graceful bamboo in the background. It was painted from life. I even painted the background color onto a piece of paper behind my still life setup. Looking back at the painting, my immediate response is to its sensation of serenity and achievement. Then I recall that when I was creating the painting, not everything was calm and collected.

There were stresses even about how to find the appropriate rocks, how to get the white to stand out enough against the background in certain areas, how to crop it appropriately . . . but, despite all this, I was able to connect to the concept through my activity, more than I realized at the time. Through the action of painting, I am given the opportunity to bond with the 'aura' of my subject, something beyond what I may be consciously aware of at the time. This relationship of conscious attention and connection to my subject, direction into action, which leads to creation, is immensely powerful. In order to create artwork, I feel I must embody the subject. In doing so, I may get caught up in details, which is normal and fine. However, I must remember to keep stepping back, in order to maintain balance and harmony through the whole composition.

I liken this experience of painting to a more general scope of perpetual thought to action in life, a reality that I became most aware of upon my first meeting with Pamela, over 10 years ago. I was in high school, experiencing true, severe depression. I had tried many therapists and what felt like every prescription drug in the pharmacy, with no real help. Therapists seemed to just sit there and sympathize while I presented my weekly dissertation of all that was wrong. Then my father came to me with Pamela's flyer—a smiling lady on a pale blue green background, with bullet points that described an approach to therapy that combined fitness. I had some positive experiences with yoga by this time. Willing to try anything, I scheduled an appointment with her. Meeting her changed everything. Immediately I knew by location that this would be something special, being that her office was inside a fitness center, as opposed to a hospital.

At the time that I saw Pamela, she was working largely with Cognitive Behavioral Therapy, supplemented by fitness exercises and meditative/awareness techniques. We would begin through discussion in her office. We would set specific achievable goals and evaluate thought processes. She supplied me with techniques to change my thoughts, which I realized, directly affected how I felt. We would then enter the exercise area, and do some light activity. I would place the new thoughts into each conscious action. This second part certainly altered the typical therapist patient relationship. The ability to conquer negative emotions through first changing a thought, then making a move, was symbolic and significant. Since this time, I have trained myself to not indulge in those negative thoughts. I actively choose new ones, which immediately affects how I feel. I have also continued going to yoga classes since that time. I may enter the class frazzled, sometimes, but the action of getting myself there, going through the motions, and consciously directing my thoughts into them, greatly alters my state, each and every time. This is the same concept—improving one's situation through awareness of the deep connection between mind and body, thought and action.

Her approach to therapy has evolved since then. However, the core methodology, which still helps me to this day, was already in place. I strongly believe that

Pamela's approach is so effective because she makes it accessible to everyone. Pamela achieves a unique balance between her sensitive, genuine, caring nature—a relationship that feels sincere, practical and achievable. Thought changes behavior, but behavior also changes thought. If I perform an exercise that makes me feel physically strong, inherently, I also feel psychologically stronger.

Part of being treated as an equal meant that thoughts, ideas, and feelings were not discriminated against. This is essential, because judging yourself due to your thoughts only brings more negative emotion. The energy should be channeled towards how to actively choose another thought, instead of wallowing, engulfed in the presence of the negative thought. So here I am, ready to share some of my thoughts and how I changed them, in the most genuine manner—because I feel that being real, too, is the best way to be.

I was filled with anxiety, as well as admitted fear, about writing this chapter. I was supposed to be writing about conquering the very problems I was experiencing. It was never the perfect time, I was never living ideally enough to be in the right state . . . to 'write,' pun intended. I never knew exactly what to say until I had no more time left and decided to read the rest of the book. I first read about the chakras on the subway ride home. This is something I had heard of for a long time, but never had given particular attention to learning in detail. As instructed by the paragraph, I took a conscious breath into each chakra described. With each breath, I felt the sensation of the chakra's meaning, simply by directing chosen thoughts into the action of my breath.

Upon arriving at my location of writing, I then read the chapter about the healing power of pets, which made me greatly miss my dear bearded dragon lizard, who I am accustomed to having by my side at night. However, simply recalling his presence brought a feeling of comfort and warmth. He has been by my side for about three years, through suffering, exploration, peace, and happiness. But I always feel happiness when I hold him.

I then proceeded to read the section about 'going within,' acknowledging the technique of grounding oneself in the pubis symphysis area. It again amazed me that each and every time I would focus on breathing into an imagined location of negative energies in my body, I felt an immediate sensation of relief and realization. If only people could become addicted to this instead.

Why is remembering to do the right thing in the moment so difficult? So easy to remember when we feel 'okay,' so difficult to recall when in that time of stress. As in painting—the time of stress when the conditions aren't perfect, the values are off, whatever it may be . . . to remember the greater picture, to recall the assembly of artistic techniques I have ingrained into my mind over the years, and to trust my innate aesthetic sense and ability to navigate a creative experience. The problem is not specifically the composition being off. If I let the stress of something veering from the ideal take over, no matter how long I keep painting, I could just make it worse. It will not all be better once this one thing is fixed. Something new will occur. What needs to change is my attitude and perspective. I need to take a step back, a conscious breath, and a reorientation through awareness of my senses. Art making, as in every activity of life, will continue to be a perpetual cycle of new challenges. One does not learn once how to fix it and then be done with it.

I have learned much from Pamela, and much about art. This doesn't mean that I will never have negative thoughts again, or I will always succeed in directing myself towards better ones. There will always be a perpetual cycle of learning, which requires maintenance, as well as growth. How we view ourselves directly affects how we feel. It is a self-fulfilling prophecy, in a way.

Sometimes we go down the wrong 'path,' but I believe there is no true right or wrong path, just a path that feels right to us, that works. There will always be obstacles on the path, mislabeled short cuts, and detours. But this is part of the journey. Seemingly things work out the way they feel they were meant to, as long as one keeps putting effort in following what drives them, what they love. I imagine striving towards a sunrise peeking through the trees of a forest. The problem is that one does not naturally appreciate it in the moment. When I create art, the situation is not always ideal when I begin, or even throughout. But I am connecting to something greater than the obstacle of that moment, through my action, such that, in retrospect, I can appreciate and understand what I've created and connected to, more.

Well here I am, doing exactly what I've just read from Pamela to do—writing about these fears, relating it to my artistic struggles, just getting it out. I am taking breaths into my being to reorient myself. I am recalling all I have learned over the years, and making it present. It is not the obstacle that needs to be overcome, it is the ability to summon the strength to live and appreciate it, as it flows through you. Without obstacles, life has no traction. Challenges and the ability to overcome them give deeper meaning to life, such that it can be genuinely fulfilling. But . . . how to do it? Well, it seems Pamela gives some pretty good advice. Is that not what we do as humans? We use our creativity to formulate methods, which designate what encompasses our existence. We can change our reality through our actions. This is our power. There is nothing to be scared of because there is nothing to be ashamed of. We can embrace the powers we deserve.

Thank you, Pamela, for the bridge you have created to that sunrise."

Part Two

Body-Mind Connection: Treating Trauma

7

Somatic Therapy

"You can't stop the waves, but you can learn to surf."
                                        –Jon Kabat-Zinn

In a short chapter I cannot even begin to give you an idea of the immense field of somatic therapy or somatic psychology and its relationship to healing trauma. The field is vast. According to the *United States Association for Body Psychotherapy*, Somatic Psychology (body-mind psychotherapy, body-oriented psychotherapy) embraces the connection between body, mind and spirit. It tends to be more experiential than talk therapy or Cognitive Behavioral Therapy. It may include meditation, mindfulness, pranayama (breathing techniques) and movement such as yoga or dance. As a former dancer, these techniques speak to my soul more than simple traditional talk therapy. The word "Soma" is Greek in origin and according to the *Dictionary of Psychology* means the body as a whole, all organic tissue, and the body as distinguished from the mind or psyche. What I intend to do is give you a simplified version of what it is to approach psychotherapy, with a focus on the body first rather than starting with the mind. I do recognize, however, that there are people who prefer solely talk therapy. The most important thing for a person to do when entering therapy for the first time is to find a therapy approach that resonates with their being.

Many clients cringe at the thought of starting therapy with a focus on the body. This is especially the case if they suffer from an eating disorder or a distorted body image, also known as body dysmorphia. It takes time, patience, courage and a non-judgmental stance to approach the body with love. Having a non-judgmental stance is easier said than done. Try for just one day to notice every time you judge yourself or someone else. You will be amazed at how often we judge. Noticing our internal sensations can help us know ourselves more and judge ourselves less.

One of the exercises Peter Levine uses to connect to bodily sensations in his book *Waking the Tiger, Healing Trauma*, is done with a shower massage. He suggests feeling the water pulsing against your skin as a way to begin noticing sensations within the body. Another exercise I like to suggest is touching your limbs to feel your body. You can actually squeeze each part of your limbs to bring more attention and awareness to them. You may begin with your feet and then move upward through your calves, knees and thighs to your hands, arms and shoulders. When you come to your arms you can give yourself a hug, which brings in self-love and bodily awareness at the same time. You can return your awareness back to your feet and begin to scan the body from the feet to the top of the head with present awareness and attention.

Most people have little awareness of the therapeutic benefits of working with the body. This is a generalization; but, in my experience, often when people enter the therapy room they expect and want to work exclusively on the mind. Some people are completely unaware of the mind-body connection and how when our mind is troubled our body too can become ill with all types of disease. In our Western culture, we are overly exposed to images in the media of perfect bodies; what people do not realize is that many photos are air brushed or retouched to look perfect. Of course, on television, the camera crews know exactly which angles to shoot for the perfect outcome. We tend to compare ourselves to this perfect model of how we are supposed to look. When we go to the gym and work out for hours to try to look like the images we see, often it does not work. We begin to get depressed and give up. The mind will mess us up every time in thinking we have to achieve the perfect body. Somatic therapy gives us an opportunity to get to know our body on a more intimate level and to appreciate it for its beauty and for all of its flaws.

One phrase I use that confuses some people is "breathe into the body." I had a yogi ask me once, "What do you mean by that?" My answer was, "To begin with, start by noticing each body part and how it feels to send the breath there. For example, if you think of breathing into the feet, visualize the feet with your eyes closed and pay close attention to any sensations in the feet. You can even wiggle each toe to get in touch with that area and then with each breath imagine the air heading down towards the feet and the feet expanding with each inhale and releasing with each exhale. In other words, as you are breathing deeply you are imagining that each body part is expanding with each in breath and relaxing with each out breath."

The quote at the beginning of the chapter by Jon Kabat-Zinn, *"You can't stop the waves, but you can learn to surf"* sums up somatic therapy nicely. The process of stabilizing the nervous system in a wavelike fashion is similar to the steadiness of a pendulum swinging back and forth. In Somatic Experiencing® this process is called *pendulation.* We learn to "pendulate" back and forth between the traumatic areas of the body and the resourced or safer areas of the body. If you think of how an infinity sign looks (a side-lying number 8), then you can picture how our healthy nervous system flows. When energy moves in this wavelike fashion, our entire being begins to relax. Before mastering this concept the first step to somatic work is to have keen body awareness.

Earlier we spoke of touching each body part. When I was a fitness trainer, a great way to get people in touch with their bodies when they were lifting weights was a technique called touch training. I would touch the muscle that they were working on gently to bring awareness to it. It always amazed me that even when touching their muscle some clients could not feel that muscle working. It was almost like the neurons that were shooting messages from the brain were not connected to that particular muscle. Growing up as a dancer I had an over awareness of my body. I felt every tiny thing and still do.

Being in touch with the body allows you to feel things viscerally and have a great intuition. It also allows you to sculpt your body more quickly with weight training because of the body-mind awareness.

How do you get this awareness if it just is not there? Practice, practice, and practice! Practice the visualization of the muscle working and the muscle fibers becoming engaged within each movement and breath. Another way to scan is to go through each muscle and contract and release it isometrically (in the same position) so that you are bringing awareness to tightening and opening. Most of what we do in yoga-psychotherapy is about contract and release or about tightening and opening. I first learned this concept in the dance world and use it currently in my psychotherapy practice. It fits into almost every aspect.

To teach body awareness I begin by asking these questions:

Where are you tight? Where do you feel open? How do you know that you are open? What can you see when you close your eyes? What do you feel? What are the physical sensations? Can you visualize your muscles and organs? Can you drop into your body and just notice? To get out of the mind can you become the witness of your thoughts instead of getting attached to them?

To summarize, somatic therapy is all about developing an awareness of and focus on the body. Body awareness is a skill that needs practice for years and years to master. Do not give up; although it may not be initially obvious the connection is there, and it is important for physical, mental and spiritual health. Be diligent and go slow and you will find your way into the body. Over time you may appreciate your insides as much as your outsides. I always used to say that I wished my insides would match my outsides. This has happened for me over time with acceptance and persistence. Maybe you want your outsides to match your insides more. Whatever the situation may be, there is hope that you can learn a new way of being with your body so that you can begin to be "whole" and have a fluid connection of the body, mind and spirit.

Psycho-tips

- Check in with your body and notice what you feel on the inside.
- Perform a body scan from the feet to the top of the head expanding on the "in" breath and releasing on the "out" breath.
- Breathe into the body, visualizing each muscle relaxing with each "out" breath— riding the wave.
- Notice what feels contracted and what feels open and focus on the open areas.
- Touch each body part to connect to it and notice how it feels to touch your body.
- Feel the sensations of the water while showering. Notice each and every drop touching your skin.
- Contract and release isometrically (without movement) each muscle to bring more awareness to the body and visualize your muscles and organs while doing this.

8

Yoga-Psychotherapy

"Yoga is the practice of tolerating the
consequences of being yourself."
                    –Bhagavad Gita

When I first became a yoga-psychotherapist, I quickly realized that no one knew what yoga-psychotherapy was. In California, it is more widely recognized; but in my neck of the woods, Fairfield County, Connecticut, it is a new field of practice.

Yoga-psychotherapy is different from *yoga therapy*. *Yoga therapy* is popularly used to treat many types of emotional healing, including trauma. It is *physiological* in nature and practiced mostly on the mat. The certifications are primarily geared towards the yoga professional. *Yoga-psychotherapy*, on the other hand, is *psychological* in nature and can only be practiced by a licensed psychotherapist (with a clinical or counseling license). It may not ever utilize a yoga mat or yoga asanas (poses).

In Chapter 14 you will learn more about Eastern traditions such as the koshas which are Hindu teachings of the five layers to get to the self. The koshas are compared to the layers of an onion; as we peel away each layer, we gain an understanding of our psychological issues. In yoga and in psychotherapy, we have the same intention of getting to our truest self. We aim for our layers of defenses to become more manageable and less needed over time.

In the study of psychology, there are hundreds of theories of how best to obtain inner peace. They all approach the "self" in a different way, but all want the same result. What I offer in this book and in my practice is a holistic, healthy, evidence-based way to achieve a peaceful existence over time. It is never easy and there are no quick fixes. It also ebbs and flows in that sometimes it works and it is great; other times you feel like you are completely starting over. That is the nature of psychotherapy. We dig deeper and deeper over time, and we are presented with greater struggles as we go inward towards our wounds and our psyches.

The risk of turning inward can result in the powerful reward of learning who we are and who we were meant to be in this existence. In the remainder of this chapter, I will attempt to share with you what it looks and feels like to come to a yoga-psychotherapy session.

Treatment

When we begin treatment, we sit and talk about the issues at hand in addition to any relevant family or trauma history you may have. In the initial sessions, we are evaluating whether or not we are a good fit for one another in a working therapeutic relationship. First impressions are not always what they seem to be and sometimes time is needed, on both sides, to develop a therapeutic bond.

Once the bond is established, I offer a more holistic approach than just simple talk therapy. This can mean adding meditation, mindfulness, or somatic work to a session. If a client is open to doing some minor yoga stretching we can do this from a chair or on a yoga mat. Meditation can also be done from a chair or the floor. In all cases the client's comfort is the priority. Many sessions are never taken to the floor; doing the somatic work, yoga, mindfulness and meditation from the couch or chair is perfectly fine and still beneficial.

When I take my sessions to the floor, the comfort level often increases. This could be because I, as a yogi, am more comfortable on the floor, and that transfers to clients. Alternatively, maybe people just have more fun on the floor. Being on the floor is more childlike and brings out an innocent, youthful, and playful side of clients. I love my practice, and I enjoy every bit of my work with clients, even when it gets rough and clients are at their worst. I always see them in their highest potential, their brightest light, and their best selves.

Sessions either on a chair or on the floor flow effort-lessly at times from talking, to checking into the body, to closed eye processes, to yoga breathing techniques, to becoming fully present, to exploring emotions and trau-mas, and to moving the body in such a way that discovery can be made. Connection can begin to happen between the body and the mind, and if the client is open to explor-ing spirituality, we add that component as well.

Exploration of the body and the mind can even be achieved through Skype and FaceTime sessions as well.

Initially it took time for me to gain comfort in this area, but now I find it valuable and worthwhile. With the world becoming more electronically connected, it has become easier to have contact with clients from all over. The work is wonderful if it can be done in person. If it cannot, the skills can still be learned across the globe. I have facilitated yoga sessions solely through Skype and FaceTime with much success. Whether the therapy is offered in person or through cyberspace, the benefits of stabilizing the nervous system through yoga, yoga-psychotherapy, or somatic therapy can be achieved.

One of my Somatic Experiencing® (SE) instructors said that with SE we are stabilizing one nervous system at a time so that we can create a ripple effect within the world. With my yoga, Somatic Experiencing®, fitness and mental health background, this ripple effect can hopefully inspire people who would have never had interest in the self-exploration of traditional therapy. There are so many aspects to therapy, and it no longer carries the traditional stigma that it is for the "sick." People who seek therapy are on the path to bettering themselves, to growing to their highest potential, and to being as healthy as they can be physically, mentally, emotionally and spiritually.

Every day there seems to be more and more research about the body-mind connection and body-mind therapies. Most recently in *Atlantic* magazine (August 24, 2016 issue) a reference was made to an article in the journal *Proceedings of the National Academy of Sciences*, where Pittsburgh neuroscientists discovered a brain-body connection through the study of the brain and the adrenal glands. Specifically, when the brain deals with emotional stress, the adrenal glands are triggered to respond and help us cope with the stress. What used to be a theory about this connection is now becoming proven in the neuroscience world. The more research that shows the connection of our brain to our body, the more widely respected the field of somatic therapies will be. There is already ample research on the benefits of meditation and mindfulness on the nervous system, and these are currently the most widespread concepts and practices of body-mind therapies.

When it comes to trauma, it is imperative to connect to the vulnerable areas within your body as slowly as possible; I like to say *"one grain of sand at a time."* In Somatic Experiencing® this is called *titration*. This work is best done with a Somatic Experiencing Practitioner (SEP). The process of slowing things down, checking in with the body and titrating into vulnerable areas can be difficult for clients. Often clients want to tell their life story before checking in with their body. They may even feel interrupted when I ask them to pause for a moment and check in with their body. The connection is awkward and disconnected for many. Just the act of stopping the story to check into what they are feeling on the inside is something that many have not been exposed to in the clinical therapy room. The first step is to take a pause in between all of the thoughts that you want to get out and check in with the body; essentially we take the focus away from the mind and onto the physical feelings.

I used this method recently with a client who told

me that he gets into so much trouble in his life because he has "no filter," meaning he says whatever is on his mind without thinking first. We worked on pausing and breathing between each sentence which was enormously frustrating on his part. However, after about a week of practicing slowing down and focusing on the breath and body, he stated having more success with becoming aware of his filter. In addition to his feeling good, his family members reported being delighted with the change!

Whereas some somatic therapies use only mindfulness, meditation and visualization, *yoga-psychotherapy* incorporates the breath and movement too. Each session is different and is tailored to the individual. I honor the work and feel blessed that I can create a safe space for people to enter with trust and help them change their lives for the better. Every individual is unique. In addition, every session offers a different approach, which keeps it new and exciting each time I meet with someone.

Psycho-tips

- Yoga and psychotherapy peel away our layers of defenses in order to get to our truest selves.
- Sessions begin in a traditional talk therapy environment until a therapeutic bond is established.
- Yoga-psychotherapy is a new field. There is ample research supporting the brain-body connection.
- Movement during sessions can enable you to get more comfortable and in touch with your body-mind connection.
- A spiritual element can be added for those who are interested in the body-mind-spirit connection.
- When sessions are taken to the floor a childlike quality can permeate.
- You can learn yoga and psychotherapeutic tools through cyberspace!

9

Going Within

"I never knew this would be so difficult!"
–Adria Knapp

"Going within" is something we say as yogis, as meditation students and as teachers. Some yogis say, "turn your focus inward" or "notice your mind's eye." Going inward or within is a scary place for many people. This is why people turn to alcohol, drugs and sex amongst other addictions: to avoid facing themselves. To go within means to be one with YOU, fully embodied and to be one with all that is. According to the late Dr. Wayne Dyer, it is the gap between the thoughts. It is the space between the lines or the silence that some might find uncomfortable. We will all at some point need to go inside to be able to fully get out of our own way. In other words, the only way out is "through" and the only way through is "in."

See if you are able to "go within" with the following exercise:

Notice how it is to just pause for a moment. Pause and feel the earth below you, the chair you are sitting on and the environment around you. Bring your full attention and awareness to the now, to this present moment. As thoughts come in and out just become a witness to the thoughts instead of getting attached to them. Once you are in the present moment and oriented to your sur- roundings you can go within. To ground yourself and bring your energy downward, bring your attention to the area between your hip bones and between your pubic bone and tailbone. Contract the muscles inward and upward like an elevator on the inhale and release the muscles upon the exhale. This will assist in initiating support, cen- tering and grounding.

Allow your eyes to close or if you prefer, keep them open with a soft gaze downward. What happens when you check in with yourself? Is there a pleasant or unpleas- ant emotion that arises? Is there an image or sensation? Is there a tightening or an opening? Notice where you feel a tightening. Without focusing on the tightening, notice if there is an area in the body that feels more open. When you get to the open area, allow yourself to stay there for a few moments to feel the opening and breathe into it by visualizing the area that you are breathing into. If your attention heads back towards the tighter areas in the body, try not to focus on them and come right back to the open areas. Enjoy the open areas as long as you can and we will explore how to approach the more difficult areas in future chapters.

When I first became a yogi, I did not have any knowl- edge of Somatic Experiencing®. Once I was introduced to the work, I realized how well it went with my psy- chotherapy practice. Yoga is about going inward through yogic philosophy and moving meditation. Somatic Experiencing® has the same intention as yoga, but with a different approach. With yoga-psychotherapy, you may be asked to "go within" during a yoga pose also known as an asana. With Somatic Experiencing® you may be asked to "go within" during a regular talk therapy session with your eyes open. It is recommended that when you do these exercises you are in the present moment. If you are in a deep meditation, approaching traumatic areas in the body is not recommended.

In yoga, breathing exercises known as pranayama are also done with the intention of going within. Unfortunately, yoga has become commercialized and a lot of the deeper meanings are lost in yoga studios and gyms where the focus is just on asanas or poses. Yoga goes much deeper than that. One of the threads (foundations) of yoga from the *Yoga Sutras of Patanjali* is "Practice becomes firmly grounded when well attended to for a long time, without break and in all earnestness." What I have found with "going within" is that if I tend to it with daily practice, I seem to be able to tolerate myself a little more each day! That is what it is all about: being able to tolerate oneself within the stillness and sacredness of life without avoidance.

What we try to do in therapy and in yoga is to get comfortable in our own skin, feel our insides, and face our demons. If this is too scary to approach you can always come out or zone out, and feel like you are rising above yourself. In clinical terms, this is called dissociation. A simpler way to describe dissociation is going to the "clouds." It is as if you are taking a break from yourself to go to a place of peace and tranquility. It sounds lovely, right? It is. I used to spend a lot of time there. However, I have learned over the years to come back to my body, to be in my body, to be fully embodied and to tolerate ME.

This brings in the questions of, "Who am I? Why am I here? What is my purpose?" What if your purpose was just to "be," not to act or do? What if the goal was to just be the most genuine YOU that you can be? Some people almost immediately find it peaceful to go inside. Others will find it impossible. When we cannot fully be comfortable with ourselves we can turn to unhealthy vices to get us through the day, the week and through life. Therefore, during a body scan when you first try to "go within," if you encounter a fearful place, come out to the "clouds" for a moment and try it again. You can always open your eyes to completely exit the scary place.

Other healthy outside resources that help us through fear may include beautiful places in nature, exquisite flowers, a lake or ocean, a mountain crest, rain, snow, trees, or anything that you find brings you peace and tranquility. Music can be a tremendous resource for finding peace within. In Zen meditation, we do it in silence. However, I meditated for 15 years with Reiki (Japanese method of healing) music and found that extremely helpful. It was not until recently that I was fully able to go into silent meditation and love and appreciate the beauty of silence. This is due to the diligent practice of "going within" daily. It is not always easy to find inner peace. Our work never ends, although it does get easier over time. It is helpful to remember that we are all on this journey together.

Think about another way of going within as an entering into yourself, your core, and your being. Full embodiment comes from a feeling of being grounded and present in each and every cell of your body. Some people live their entire lives feeling disembodied. Almost like zombies, they just go from one thing to the next without having any present awareness. Their lives can be like a time bomb ready to explode because their stress levels are so high; or alternatively, they are like the Energizer Bunny, always moving to avoid their inner self and eventually running out of capacity and dropping from exhaustion. Both of these ways are not healthy for the nervous system and ultimately become issues over time.

Remembering to begin the process of awareness and mindfulness with small steps will help you later to attain a fuller presence over time. The Yoga Sutra teaches us about the benefits of sustained practice. With repetition we can train our brains, our muscles and our nervous systems how to relax and just be. We can train ourselves to slow down and actually enjoy the space between the lines, the gap between the thoughts and our pure essence within.

Psycho-tips

- Notice how it feels to just take a pause without judgment.
- What do you feel like on the inside as you land in your body?
- If the inside is scary with your eyes closed, then keep them open and just gaze downward.
- If the inside is still scary, exit and imagine going to the "clouds" while you continue to check in with your body. (You may also exit the areas of fear by noticing beautiful places in nature, exquisite flowers, a lake or ocean, a mountain crest, rain, snow, trees, an animal, a crystal or anything else that makes you feel safe.)
- Come back in towards your being at a slow pace, for just a few seconds to begin.
- Notice what it feels like to be inside and to be fully embodied.
- Welcome yourself to YOU and acknowledge your presence without judgment.

10

Pranayama: Breathing Exercises
(pra-na-ya-ma)

"Presence itself breathes through me, the unseen
substance of love so tangible and strong that
each long breath offers up the key to my release."
—Danna Faulds

There are many different types of breaths which can be used in a therapy session or a yoga class. I offer a brief description of a few and encourage you to try a beginning yoga class if you never have. Injuries can occur during yoga. Therefore, it is most important to start with an introductory class that is geared toward the total novice. Yoga is not about competition or getting it right. It is about getting in touch with your inner truth.

Below are some breaths that may be beneficial for you:

Yoga Breath: Belly Breath

A traditional yoga breath is similar to a diaphragm breath that singers use to strengthen their vocal abilities. It is also called a belly breath or a three part breath. The three parts are the belly, the ribs and the heart. On the inhale you fill the belly, ribs and heart as if you are filling up a balloon and expanding your chest to a V shape. The lower abdomen fills and expands below the naval and the lower back expands as well. The ribs and heart expand outward from front to back as if you are three dimensional. (This has also been called a three dimensional breath.) The overall concept is to expand on the inhale and deflate on the exhale while allowing your shoulders to remain relaxed and away from your ears. It is also calming to visualize bringing in all the good in the universe on the inhale and letting out all the stress on the exhale, sending it either upward toward the universe or down into the earth. As long as you are sending the stress and negativity away from you upon the exhale, you are inviting in peace.

Ujjayi Breath: Victory Breath
(u-jja-yi)

This is my favorite breath and the one I use when teaching either gentle Vinyasa (yoga that flows and feels to me like a dance) or more vigorous Vinyasa (a flow that ads an element of cardio-vascular exercise because of the faster movements). The Ujjayi breath is also called the Victory breath; it sounds like the waves of the ocean or the ominous breathing of Darth Vader in *Star Wars*. I think everyone loves this breath, especially the teens I see in my private practice. It is a deep breath in and out through the nose that lands in the back of the throat and has a loud sound that is like a snore. This breath drowns out recurring thoughts and allows you to clear your head and come into the present moment. It is grounding and centering and can cause a state of peaceful acceptance and non-judgment. It is very yogi! In fact, the breath during the asanas (postures) actually can take your yoga practice to a deeper level of inner connection and meaning. If you are new at yoga, the Ujjayi breath can take your focus off of the uncomfortable muscles and onto the breath itself; it creates prana or life force energy. *Yoga is all about the breath . . . as is life!*

Kapalabahti: Breath of Fire
(ka-pa-la-bha-ti)

The first time I was introduced to this breath, I was in my twenties and in a hot yoga class. Hot yoga is done in a studio with a temperature of 103–105 degrees. I did not mind the heat back then, but now the strain of holding the postures for an entire minute for the first set and 30 seconds for the second set can be challenging for my aging body. It was my favorite form of yoga back in my twenties.

The purpose of Kapalabahti is to detox and cleanse the mind and body. It can also help give you energy and release negative emotions. At the end of my first hot yoga class when I was on my knees doing two sets of thirty Kapalabahti in front of the mirror (hot yoga can be done in front of a mirror unlike other forms of yoga), I saw an outline, an aura of complete white light on everyone in the room; it extended upward above people's heads and was similar to what you would see in a statue of Lakshmi (Hindu Goddess of abundance). It was magical. It was worth going to class a few times a week just to see if I could notice the white light again during the Kapalabahti.

To explain this complicated breath, it is as if you are pumping the balloon of your belly so that it is filled with air, and letting it out with rapid exhalations through the nose or mouth as you push inward from the naval to the spine. Another way to describe it is that it has short exhalations followed by passive inhalations. (This breath is contraindicated for people with high blood pressure, glaucoma, epilepsy, menstruation and recent abdominal surgery. Also, any hot yoga class is not recommended for people with high blood pressure.) This breath of fire creates warmth and is especially good for bringing heat to your body during practice in the winter time. The breath is difficult to master just from reading about it because it is intense and powerful. Do this when you find a yoga class that is right for you. While not for everyone, I list it because of its detoxification benefits and its ability to bring heat to the body.

Nadi Shodhana: Alternate Nostril Breathing (na-di-sho-dha-na)

Nadi Shodhana is known to help calm the mind and bring about inner peace. It can help clear out any blocked channels of energy in the body, much like Reiki which is a Japanese technique for stress reduction and healing. Its effect is similar to acupuncture, which is an ancient Chinese technique for healing. According to Sanskrit, the ancient language of India, "Nadi" means subtle energy channel and "Shodhana" means cleaning and purification. This breath is quiet and subtle and is not recommended to be forced or loud. It can help prepare you for meditation. You can be seated comfortably with your spine erect either in a regular chair, a meditation chair or on a meditation pillow. First use your right thumb to close off your right nostril and exhale fully from the left nostril. Now to start Nadi Shodhana inhale from the left nostril keeping the right nostril closed, and then exhale from the right nostril keeping the left one closed with your right index finger. Repeat a few times inhaling from the left and exhaling from the right. You can then reverse the direction and breathe in through the right and out through the left. You do not have to switch hands to reverse this. Traditionally the breath is repeated 9 times on each side, although you can do a lower amount and still reap the benefits from this breath.

Depression Breath: 2:1 Breathing

While seated comfortably or standing, inhale for a count of four and exhale for a count of two (counting one-one-thousand, two-one-thousand). The important part of this breath is that the inhalation is deeper and longer than the exhalation. This brings life and prana (energy) to your depressed system. You can also do a longer count and pause at the top of the breath before the exhalation.

Anxiety Breath: 1:2 Breathing
(adapted from Bo Forbes, PsyD)

While seated comfortably or standing, inhale for a count of two and exhale for a count of four (counting one-one-thousand, two-one-thousand). What is important about this breath is that the exhalation is deeper and longer than the inhalation in order to expel anxiety and stress. Once again you can do a longer count and pause at the top of the breath before the exhalation.

I invite you to inhale this poem that I had written for one of my first yoga classes where I was a guest teacher:

One Breath

One breath is all it takes to be back to me
One breath to take me back home

The stillness of the breath releases
the worry that I often feel

The sound of the breath . . . like an ocean
reminding me that life is supposed to be peaceful

One breath is all it takes to find the Divine within

Carry me on the breath through the
clouds to the heavens

And stay with me so that I can take that heavenly
feeling with me wherever I go

Remind me to just take one breath so that I can
feel heaven on earth

And always be with me so that I can tap into
your holiness at any time

One breath . . . it only takes one breath to
bring us back home

In summary, the breath is the main component of yoga, meditation, mindfulness and many other techniques for healing. The breath provides the ability to connect to the earth, your being, nature, spirit, the universe or God. My hope for you is that you find a yoga class where the emphasis is on the breath and going within to find your true essence.

Psycho-tips

- Start with an introductory or beginning yoga class if you are new at this.
- Try the yoga three part breath, also called a belly breath, for grounding.
- My favorite breath, the Ujjayi breath (ocean or *Darth Vader* breath), can quiet your thoughts. It can also be done throughout your yoga practice.
- It is not recommended to perform Kapalabahti, the Breath of Fire, unless you are in a yoga class in the care of a qualified professional.
- To calm your mind you can try Nadi Shodhana, alternate nostril breathing.
- To help with depression, use 2:1 breathing.
- To help with anxiety, use 1:2 breathing. (adapted from Bo Forbes, PsyD)

11

Yoga, a Philosophy:
The Eight Limbs of Yoga

*"The Yoga we practice is not for ourselves alone,
but for the Divine; its aim is to work out the will
of the Divine in the world, to effect a spiritual
transformation and to bring down a divine
nature and a divine life into the mental, vital,
and life of humanity."*
                              –Sri Aurobindo

In modern day yoga, the emphasis is often solely on the physical aspect of yoga which is called Hatha yoga. Yoga is much more than this. It is an ancient philosophy and practice of the mind, body and spirit. It is also a devotional practice of finding the God or Goddess within. Yoga is everywhere and it is not just about postures. That is just one aspect of yoga. Below are the different paths of yoga recognized in the ancient Hindu scripture, *The Bhagavad Gita.*

The Different Paths of Yoga

Hatha yoga, yoga of postures

Raja yoga, yoga of self-control

Karma yoga, yoga of service

Jnana yoga, yoga of the mind

Bhakti yoga, yoga of devotion

Tantra yoga, yoga of rituals

Marga yoga, yoga of meditation—
path to enlightenment

Mantra yoga, yoga of vibrations

Nada yoga, yoga through sound

During my 200 hour yoga certification, I was out to dinner with friends one evening and one of them asked me if yoga was a religion. He asked this because his church would not allow yoga to be practiced in their facility. I initially told him that yoga is not a religion. While studying the *Yoga Sutras of Patanjali,* I learned that one of the definitions of yoga is the union between our mind and God's mind. I later repeated to him that yoga is not a religion, but I added that it has a huge spiritual element to it. It is also often defined as the union of mind, body and spirit. At my synagogue where I am lucky to be able to teach yoga, I have the liberty of bringing in some religion into my class and I tell people about the union between us and God. In essence, yoga can help us attain holiness and connection to the brightest, most loving parts of ourselves.

Yoga for me has been my truest connection to God. The quote from Sri Aurobindo at the beginning of this chapter speaks of this concept. It is about bringing a divine nature into humanity. Yoga is about non-judgment, connection to spirit, universe or God, taming the ego, being the best human you can possibly be, harnessing the mind, having integrity, living a life of purity, and finding your true purpose for existence. It is about clearing the mind and being in a moving meditation while you access the wonderful information within. It is a connection with the body through the breath that most other forms of therapy do not give us. Challenge yourself to do your morning stretches the yogi way, with the breath drowning out the thoughts, with an intention of going beyond your own needs and thinking of global needs, and with the hope that the stillness and peace you create within your yoga practice can be extended and permeated throughout the suffering world. We pray for positive change and for the yoga to have a domino effect on the world.

A concise description of the eight limbs of yoga follows as per the *Yoga Journal*:

"In Patanjali's *Yoga Sutras*, the eightfold path is called *ashtanga*, which literally means "eight limbs." These eight steps act as guidelines on how to live a meaningful and purposeful life. They serve as a prescription for moral and ethical conduct and self-discipline; they direct attention toward one's health; and they help us to acknowledge the spiritual aspects of our nature."

Included are descriptions for the eight limbs of yoga:

The Eight Limbs of Yoga

1. YAMAS (ya-mas)—Ethical behavior one should follow every day

Ahimsa (a-him-sa)—Non-harm to self or others
Satya (sa-tya)—Loving honesty
Asteya (a-ste-ya)—Non-stealing
Brahmacharya (bra-hma-cha-rya)—Non-excess
Aparigraha (a-pa-ri-gra-ha)—Non-attachment

2. NIYAMAS (ni-ya-mas)—Personal Observances

Saucha (sou-cha)—Body as a temple
Santosa (san-to-sha)—Humble and content
Tapas (ta-pas)—Disciplined commitment
Svadhayaya (swa-dhya-ya)—Self study
Ishvarapranidhana (i-shwa-ra-pra-ni-da-na)—
Letting go of ego

3. ASANA (a-sa-na)—Posture

4. PRANAYAMA (pra-na-ya-ma)—Breath control

5. PRATYAHARA (pra-tya-ha-ra)—Sense withdrawal

6. DHARANA (dha-ra-na)—Concentration

7. DHYANA (dyha-na)—Meditation

8. SAMADHI (sa-ma-dhi)—Contemplation or bliss

—Sri Swami Satchidananda,
The Yoga Sutras of Patanjali

The bottom line is: Be the best person you can be, have altruistic behaviors, treat your neighbors as you would want to be treated, practice loving kindness, give generously of your heart, be humble, treat yourself, everyone and everything around you with holiness and respect, detach from your ego thoughts, be genuine, be kind, be caring and compassionate and non-judgmental. That is all! It's not too much to ask!

May your practice be fulfilling and enlightening and may you continue to strive for the best YOU that you can be.

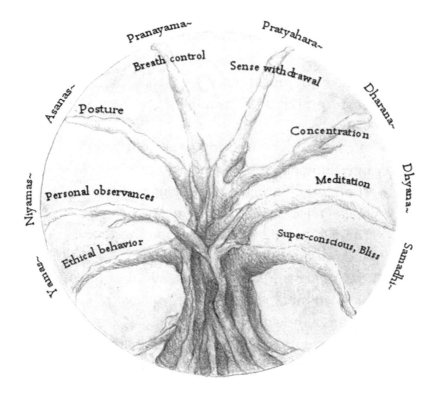

Figure 1: The Eight Limbs of Yoga

Psycho-tips

- Yoga is not just about the physical postures, it is a philosophy for purposeful living.
- Yoga allows you to bring a spiritual nature into humanity.
- There are multiple paths of yoga which make it accessible to everyone.
- The *Eight Limbs of Yoga* include the *Yamas* and *Niyamas*.
- The *Yamas* and *Niyamas* are about ethical behavior and personal observances.
- Yoga is a moving meditation.
- We strive to be the most genuine, loving, compassionate person we can be through our yoga practice.

Part Three

East and West: Combating Trauma

12

50 Practices for Healing

"A happy life cannot be without a measure of darkness, and the word happy would lose its meaning if it were not balanced by sadness."
–Carl Jung

Instead of our usual Psycho-tips at the end of the chapter, below is a list of strategies that I created for a presentation I gave on conquering depression. This is a conglomeration of my personal methods, my mentor's methods, supervisor's methods and methods I use in my practice. To conquer your deeper psychological issues and traumas, you will need to do somatic work over time with an experienced practitioner. When I say "over time" I mean over a lifetime. I do not mean to discourage you, but this is our life's work. The work never stops. By employing the many strategies you may be able to go deeper and deeper as you heal, grow and change. This is a good thing!

More Depression and Anxiety Strategies (adapted from *Conquering Teen Depression, Navigating Around the Pressures of Social Media*), presented to the Jewish Community Center in Stamford, Connecticut, 2015:

- Place your worries in a God box, prayer box or universe box and hand them over to God or the universe to take care of for you. (This will be covered more in Chapter 23, Surrender.)
- Place your sadness, depression or anxiety in an imaginary container or box and place the box at the end of the universe until you are able to tolerate being closer to it. Some of my clients have used visuals of a metal or platinum box being placed on a star or a cloud, or a black garbage bag being placed in the center of the earth. Over time we can begin to come closer to the edges of the container in order to integrate and tolerate some of our emotions attached to it. We do this slowly, turning towards our emotions only *"one grain of sand"* at a time.
- Construct a mind movie (with PowerPoint or any other movie software) with lots of happy photos, affirmations, and prayers to recite and watch daily (adapted from Dave Asomaning, PhD).
- Use the Positive Psychology technique of using negative emotions such as anger, envy, loneliness and guilt as a means to discover what the underlying issues are. Once awareness is brought to the issues, you can begin to tackle them.
- Rituals—Have a sacred space for meditation or prayer—cozy with pillows or whatever attracts you.
- Drawing an Angel Card (which is a positive affirmation card) can be beneficial. I do this with clients at the end of therapy sessions. Most of my

decks are from Doreen Virtue, PhD and include *Mermaids and Dolphins*, *Fairies*, *Goddesses*, *Archangel Michael*, and *Ascended Masters*. My clients also like *Animal Spirit Cards* from Steven D. Farmer, *Horse Spirit Cards* from Melisa Pearce and *Zen Cards* from Daniel Levin.

- Lighting candles (even fake ones for ambiance) can create a peaceful, serene and safe space.
- Using essential oils or fragrances that you love can help change your mood and outlook. I like *Peace Potion* from *White Sage* (whitesagewellness.com).
- Burning white sage (smudging) is an ancient Native American tradition that is known to clear out negative energy.
- Playing music that inspires you will potentially be uplifting.
- Bathing with sea salts or Epsom salts and adding a cup of white vinegar for extra cleansing can help to clean out your energy and aura and relax any tense muscles you may have.
- Cleaning your drawers, your house, your space, your closets, and your attic can help to diminish clutter in your spirit. Every time you clean, visualize cleaning your soul.
- TRUST that the universe will provide for you and love yourself as if you were an adorable child.
- Meditate to clear any negative karma.
- Reach out to all your supports (family, friends, loved ones) and help someone you love.

- RESOURCE—Visualize things or places that make you feel safe or hold a crystal, religious symbol, flower, or anything else that resonates with your spirit.
- Remember FAITH in times of despair . . . look for something that can give you HOPE.
- Stay in the present moment by tuning into your surroundings, paying attention and breathing.
- Use all 5 senses to come into the present moment. Observe, feel, smell, taste and hear what is around you.
- Pay attention to where your body is in space to come to the present moment. Feel your feet on the floor, grounded to the earth. Feel your spine erect and your shoulders down and back to open your heart.

Note—if you are using crystals as a resource for grounding or meditation, there is a wonderful book called *Healing Crystals and Gemstones* by Bohmer and Schreiber, that has beautiful photos of each crystal and describes their healing qualities.

The next list of strategies is taken directly from my website under the articles section (www.PamelaTinkham.com). It was written in 2007 during a time when I was a director of a weight loss program at a physician's office and offered fitness training in combination with Cognitive Behavioral Therapy (CBT) to clients.

- Set short-term goals.
- Make a plan.
- Journal your progress.
- Dispute negative thoughts.
- Have "me time" every day.
- Be organized.
- Share your goals with someone important to you so that you are accountable.
- Figure out what is fun for you and do it at least once a day.
- Do some form of exercise every day and begin and end with yoga breathing techniques.
- S . . . T . . . R . . . E . . . T . . . C . . . H . . . every day.
- Eat right with plenty of colorful fruits and vegetables.
- Watch your fat intake . . . especially saturated fat.
- Hydrate with water as often as possible.
- Find a physical activity that feels more like play than work and do it as much as possible.
- Have a gratitude journal where you write what you are grateful for on a daily basis.
- Don't compare yourself to others . . . we are all special.
- Challenge yourself physically and mentally.
- Allow yourself to have your negative feelings . . . just don't get stuck on them.
- Try to always do the right thing.
- Take a deep breath before reacting.
- 5 minutes of working out every day is better than no minutes.

- Get a good night's sleep every night.
- Watch your alcohol intake (think moderation).
- Live in the moment.
- Love as many living things as possible.
- Take care of your health.
- Watch out for fear . . . don't let it get the best of you.
- Be optimistic, laugh, and don't take life too seriously.
- Perform acts of kindness without needing recognition and give without expecting reciprocation.
- Be generous financially, generous with your spirit and heart, and hug someone at least once a day!

In summary, this is merely a suggestive list of coping strategies. For longer term success, you may need to work with a qualified individual or group who can help you dig deeper into your psychological wounds or traumas in order to heal. With appropriate care and the proper tools, you may restore your system back to wholeness.

13

To Medicate or Not

"There is no one right way, but many ways to do right."

—Betsy Kempner, MHA, BSN

In deciding whether to medicate or not, it is necessary to assess whether a major depressive disorder (a clinical, debilitating depression) or generalized anxiety disorder (overwhelming fear and anxiety) is ruining your life. When you are sick with an infection, a virus or a cold, you take medications. If you have a disease, you take medication. There is no shame in taking medication. Depression and anxiety are illnesses that need to be medicated when severe symptoms are occurring. One good way to assess whether you should go for a psychiatric evaluation is to ask yourself if your depression or anxiety is diminishing your ability to function in life. This is similar in approach to a substance abuse issue. When substance abuse interferes with your daily functioning and your ability to live your life to the fullest and relate to others, then it is time to look at the issue more closely. Also, when traumatic symptoms are severe and the skills in Chapter 12 are not working, it may be a good idea to medicate temporarily until you are able to tolerate some of the unpleasant emotions.

Challenge yourself to release all guilt and shame and to know that we all have skeletons, and we all have to face our darkness at some point in our life. It takes courage to enter the therapy or psychiatry room to begin to conquer your depression, anxiety or traumatic symptoms, but it is a positive pro-active first step.

When I was in my twenties and thirties, I was anti-medication unless severe symptoms were occurring; I instead chose to use fitness, yoga, and meditation to help conquer anxiety and depression within my clientele. I even gave lectures discouraging people from taking meds and encouraging them instead to use exercise as an anti-depressant. I now feel differently about the subject.

In my practice I have had many clients who were greatly affected by hormone imbalances and biological depression. Since then I have changed my views on the issue of medication, and I am sending more and more people for psychiatric evaluations once a physical examination has ruled out any health issues such as thyroid dysfunction or other medical reasons for the depression. I currently have a lot more respect for medication when needed and a lot more compassion for people who have "tried everything" and gone in circles in therapy, but need something more.

I am grateful to have studied at the Somatic Experiencing® Trauma Institute SE™ where I learned tools other than medication to deal with major depression and anxiety. The therapy I offer to clients now goes deeper into the wounds, and more and more people whom I treat with depression and anxiety are getting better faster. The trauma work is difficult, but is extraordinary. The breakdowns are intense, but the breakthroughs are immense! If medication is not indicated or desired, there is much we can do to guide the healing process.

Psycho-tips

- There is no shame in taking medication.
- If you are sick with an infection, cold
  or a virus, you may take medication.
  Depression is also a serious illness that
  may need to be treated with medication.
- If your depression, anxiety or traumatic
  symptoms are ruining your life, a psychiatric evaluation is indicated.
- If your depression, anxiety or traumatic
  symptoms are mild to moderate, Chapter
  12 offers many coping mechanisms.
- Everyone suffers to a certain extent. We
  CAN manage and minimize the suffering
  we have to endure.
- It is our attitude towards our suffering
  that makes or breaks us.
- If you are having any thoughts of hurting
  yourself or someone else, call 911 or
  go to the nearest emergency room.

14

Chakras, Bhandas, and Koshas

"The more you gloat, the less you actually have . . . as eternal happiness can only be found in the soul."
                              –Unknown

Some find it helpful to incorporate more spiritual ways to deal with depression and anxiety. Categorizing chakras, bhandas and koshas into one chapter do an injustice to the depth required for each of these Eastern philosophies. As an overview, I will share with you what I discuss in therapy sessions. The drawings will help show the concepts and simplify the theory.

The Chakras

Chakras (cha-kras or sha-kras) have their origins in ancient yogic and Hindu teachings. They originated about 4,000 years ago. The word "chakra" in Sanskrit (the ancient language of India) means wheel, and it refers to the wheels of energy throughout the body, each one with its own color. The colors from the tailbone to the top of the head, or the crown chakra, are the colors of the rainbow: red, orange, yellow, green, blue, indigo, and violet.

Each color represents a different emotion and intention. The purpose of yoga, meditation and Reiki, amongst other healing modalities, is to allow the energy to flow through each of the chakras. There are sounds and chants that go along with each chakra as well. In the upcoming chakra meditation each chakra will be more fully explored for its meaning and emotion. I love working with the chakras, because color brings me joy. The chakras have always resonated with me even though they are more spiritual and energy focused than scientific. There is an immense body of literature written about them.

After 15 years of studying the chakras, I thought I knew a great deal about each chakra. To my surprise, during a conversation with my friend, Sharat, I was informed that the heart chakra utilizes the *Star of David* as its symbol. I had to go over my notes when I returned home to notice that within the beautiful green symbol, if you look deeply, you can see the *Star of David*. Later, Sharat sent me an explanation from *A Joseph Campbell Companion, Reflections on the Art of Living* where it describes that the upward pointed triangle in the six pointed star within the heart chakra symbolizes aspiration and the downward pointed triangle symbolizes the obstacles that get in our way. Campbell explains how the obstacles can actually be the opening to our transformation.

Please see Figure 2 on the following page for a view of the power of color within the chakras:

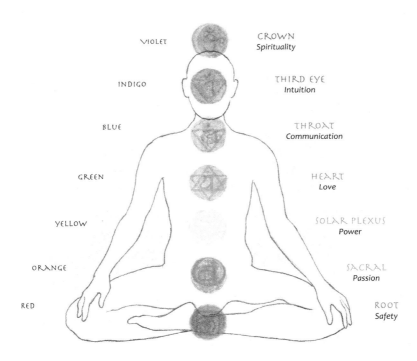

Figure 2: The Chakras

The following is one of my favorite chakra meditations along with a mantra (repeated word or phrase) for each chakra and the emotional energy associated with each chakra. By unblocking the chakras, the belief is that you will have emotional, physical, mental and spiritual peace. I especially like doing this chakra meditation at the beach; and I vary the words, phrases and mantras for that location. When I guide the meditation, I do not read from the script. I guide the meditation by allowing the meditation to be guided to me and through me.

Chakra Meditation
(Allow yourself to sit comfortably or to lie down.)

Notice the environment, the temperature of the air, the sounds, the smells and the beauty of the stillness.

Gently allow your eyes to soften or close. Begin to pay attention to your breath. Allow yourself to open with each "in" breath and release with each "out" breath.

Bring your awareness to your spine, your shoulders, your tailbone, your sitting bones and below to your legs, feet and the earth.

Feel the sand below you as a cushion of support, comfort and safety. Allow your shoulders to relax . . . lengthen tall enough so that you feel as though there is an imaginary string coming out the top of your head and pulling you upward towards the universe.

If thoughts are coming in and out, just allow those thoughts to occur without attachment to them and without judgment. Imagine that you are rising above the thoughts and witnessing them as they come in and out.

If you continue to feel attached to your thoughts, you can try to imagine them inside a big bubble just floating away into the ocean. If they continue, you may try to take an imaginary broom to sweep them away.

Bringing your awareness to the space between your hip bones and between your tail bone and pubic bone, imagine the color red as you connect to your root, your sense of safety. You may even contract the muscles in this area on the inhale to allow the energy to flow upward like an elevator and then relax the muscles on the exhale.

Continuing your attention on the red area, your root chakra, notice the flow of circular energy as you begin to feel that all your needs are taken care of. Allow yourself to stay with that feeling of safety for a few moments.

The Sanskrit name for the root chakra is "Muladhara" (mu-la-dha-ra). The sound of the root chakra is Lam and this chakra is related to finding your sense of safety and security.

Invite yourself to repeat the mantra:

"I am safe and secure in my own skin."

Traveling upward to the second chakra, which is right below your belly button, imagine a beautiful orange sunset. The Sanskrit name is Svadisthana (swa-dhi-shta-na) and the sound is Vam. This is your passion center. This chakra expresses your sensuality, sexuality and creativity. If you are not having sexual relations, making sure you are doing something creative and passionate with your life will allow this chakra to open. Invite yourself to feel your inner passion and repeat the mantra:

"I am sexy and I know it!"

Traveling up to the third chakra, which is right below your breast bone, the color is yellow like the sun which shines on the beautiful water. The Sanskrit name is Manipura (ma-ni-pu-ra) and the sound is Ram. This is your power center, your confidence and self-esteem. You tap into this chakra when you do Warrior Poses. Your personal power and strong sense of self will allow this chakra to open more fully. The mantra is:

"I am a Warrior King or Goddess."

Coming to the beautiful heart chakra, brilliant emerald green or the color of the trees after the rain has penetrated the forest, notice your heart and open to your inner-self and to others. The Sanskrit name is Anahata (a-na-ha-ta) and the sound is Yam. Allow yourself to feel love no matter what you have been feeling in the past. Breathe into the heart and allow that love to permeate inside your being, outside yourself, out to the world and to the entire universe. The mantra for this chakra is:

"I love myself; the good, the bad, and the ugly."

Taking the energy upward to the throat chakra and the back of the neck brings awareness to your voice, your inner most truth, your most genuine self and the divine message coming through you. The color is blue and the image is that of the pure blue water in the Caribbean. The Sanskrit name is Visuddha (vi-shu-ddha) and the sound is Ham. Opening your voice and your truth will allow you to live a life of divine purpose and authenticity. The mantra is:

"I speak my truth with loving compassion."

Moving toward the space between your eyebrows, the sixth chakra is the third eye chakra which is your sixth sense. This is your ability to see what cannot be seen and feel in your viscera what you already know is true. The color is indigo and it is brilliant, radiant and filled with the most magnificent blue/purple glow. The Sanskrit name is Ajna (a-gya) and the sound is the universal sound of "Om" (ohm). Breathe love and light into this chakra as the mind becomes even calmer and the stillness allows you to open to greater insight and possibilities. The mantra is:

"I can see clearly now."

Lastly we reach the crown chakra at the top of your head which is violet with white light above it permeating out to the universe. As you open up to the universe you can allow the flow of energy to come to you and through you. You can also let go of any unwanted tension by sending it up and out to the universe. The aim is to remain peaceful and tranquil in your skin. The Sanskrit name for the crown chakra is Sahasrara (sa-ha-sra-ra) and the sound is also the universal sound of "Om." Sending love and light out to the universe and receiving blessings of abundance and peace, you may repeat the mantra:

"I connect to spirit, the universe (and God, if that is your belief) and shine my love and light on the world."

As you go through each chakra, notice that your breath will feel more alive and full. Imagine the elevator we spoke of earlier stemming from the root chakra and allow the "in" breath to go all the way from there and flow upwards through the crown and into the universe. On the "out" breath imagine that the breath is coming down from the universe bringing all the beautiful divine energy into your being, entering through the crown, traveling through each chakra and finally down into the earth. As you breathe deeply, begin to come back to the present moment by noticing the air temperature as the light breeze touches your skin. Notice your body and the sounds around you. Allow yourself to be fully present, here in this moment while you begin to move each finger and each toe.

The next three breaths will begin to deepen your awareness in the present moment and bring you back to your body with each part of you being alive with radiant energy. Notice your limbs, your seat, your belly and ribs, your chest, your lower and upper back, your neck and head and breathe deeply into the belly so that you expand your being and release with a gentle "ha" sound.

For the next part of the meditation, I invite you to repeat these phrases to yourself or out loud with your hands in prayer. (*Anjali Mudra*—a hand position that will be covered in Chapter 15.) The following is a traditional Buddhist Metta (Loving Kindness) meditation:

May we be safe
May we be sound
May we be free from pain and suffering
May we have peace

May you be safe
May you be sound
May you be free from pain and suffering
May you have peace

May they be safe
May they be sound
May they be free from pain and suffering
May they have peace

Thank you for allowing me to guide you during this chakra meditation. At the end of a meditation or yoga class we traditionally bow out with our hands in prayer (Anjali Mudra) and say the word Namaste (nah-mas-tay). We bow first to the teacher within us and then to our other classmates to acknowledge the teacher within them.

Namaste's meaning can be translated as:

The divine light in me honors the divine light in you.

Namaste . . .

The Bhandas

The bhandas (bon-das) can be described as energy locks in the body. Releasing each bhanda will ignite energy throughout the body with greater power than the gentler chakras. In engaging the *Mula Bhanda,* which is the perineum, or space between the tailbone and pubic bone, it involves contracting the muscles between the hip bones, pubic bone and tailbone; it is similar to a kegal exercise where the contraction can be viewed as pulling the energy inward and upward like an elevator. Upon the release imagine your energy flowing more freely. Contracting the *Mula Bhanda* at the beginning of a meditation can help you find grounding and your connection to the earth.

The *Uddiyana Bhanda,* which is actually used in almost every form of fitness, is when you pull your belly button toward the spine. In Pilates (a series of low-impact exercises) there is the concept of "scooping" the belly button to the spine. This is to engage the intra-abdominal muscles and work them more fully. The Pilates concept is similar to the *Uddiyana Bhanda*, although with the bhandas we work with energy and with Pilates we work with the core muscles.

The *Jalandhara Bhanda* is a lock of the throat. It can be engaged during certain yoga asanas (postures) or simply by tucking your chin to your chest and engaging the breath in an inward and upward motion.

If you engage all three bhandas at once, it is referred to as *Maha Bhanda*.

Please see Figure 3 on the following page to observe the bhandas within the body:

Maha Bhanda

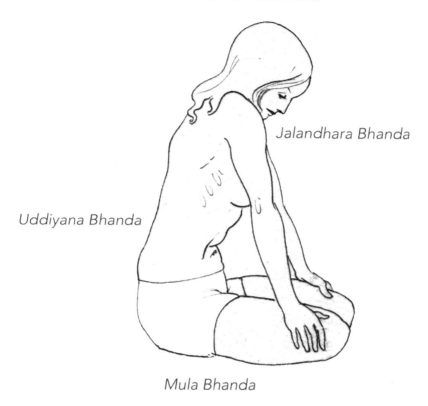

Jalandhara Bhanda

Uddiyana Bhanda

Mula Bhanda

Figure 3: The Bhandas

The Koshas

The koshas (ko-shas) are known as the five layers of being and are referred to as sheaths in the Hindu tradition. If you visualize the layers of an onion and how you can peel away each layer to get to the center, that is how the koshas work. I refer to them in my psychotherapy sessions often because therapy is all about peeling away our layers of defenses to get to our truth. The outer layer of the onion is called the *Annamaya Kosha* which has to do with the physical body. The next layer, the *Pranamaya Kosha,* deals with our energy. Moving inwards towards our core is the *Manomaya Kosha*, the mental layer. This layer can get in our way of finding our truest self. Once we can get past this layer, we can enter the wisdom layer which is the *Vijnanamaya Kosha*. After this layer comes bliss, the *Anandamaya Kosha,* which is then followed by the inner circle of the imaginary onion and is called the "self."

During our quest for enlightenment we can enter the inner layers, but find we may be bounced back to the outer layers when life gets tough. We strive to stay within, but our mind, circumstances and other issues take us back out constantly. Even the most enlightened of beings are not able to stay within permanently. To be present on a moment-to-moment basis it takes commitment and continued practice.

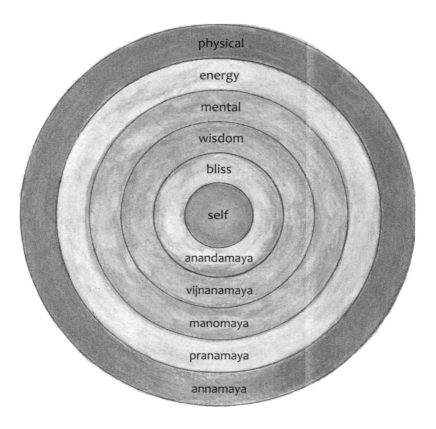

Figure 4: The Koshas

Psycho-tips

- The chakras are wheels of energy throughout the body.
- They are the colors of the rainbow from the tailbone to the crown.
- A chakra meditation can be very soothing, especially when practiced in a beautiful place in nature.
- The bhandas are energy locks in the body.
- If you engage the chakras and the bhandas, you can ignite your flow of energy and remove obstacles and blocks of stuck energy. The obstacles within may be an opening to our transformation.
- The koshas are a sheath around the "self" and are comparable to layers of an onion and our layers of defenses.
- Psychotherapy, somatic therapy, yoga-psychotherapy, mindfulness and meditation amongst other healing modalities will assist you in peeling away layers of defenses in order to get to your most authentic self, your truth, and your bliss which can assist you in restoring and repairing traumatic issues.

15

Meditation and Mindfulness

"Within the silence we find everything. Take the time to enjoy it. You might find out who you are, who you will be, and find how far you have come or need to go."

–John Hodge, A.C.E.

Meditation

When people think of meditation, they sometimes have a preconceived notion that it is something done in white robes in a monastery or a secluded place. It is true that isolation can make it easier to meditate, especially without the stress of dealing with family members, partners, children or spouses on a daily basis. However, we live in the real world along with the challenges of interpersonal relationships. Therefore, it is in our best interest to learn how to incorporate meditation in that environment. Meditation does not necessarily mean sitting crossed legged and chanting "OM." In fact, once you master the skills, you can consider life itself a moving meditation.

There are many forms of meditation, but for this book to be an inspiration and not intimidation, I will keep it very simple. Take ten deep breaths in the morning and ten at night. There you go! You are a pro!

There is ample research on the benefits of meditation and how to begin a practice. *The Meditative Mind: The Varieties of Meditative Experience* by Daniel Goleman (author of Emotional Intelligence) and *Buddha's Brain: The Practical Neuroscience of Happiness, Love and Wisdom* by Rick Hanson are both great books if you would like to explore further.

Simply stated, meditation is a practice of turning inward. It may be done with eyes open or closed and involves tuning into YOU, your spirit self, your connection to nature or to the universe or God. It is the practice of "Stopping and dropping into the body" as Jon Kabat-Zinn stated.

In yoga and in therapy, we sit comfortably and choose a hand position which is called a mudra in Sanskrit, which means a seal, mark or gesture. If we sit with our palms facing upward, we are asking to receive something. If we place our hands downward on our legs, we are attempting to ground and center ourselves. If we place our index finger and thumb together with palms up, we are in Chin Mudra or Gayan Mudra. In yoga, the thumb is symbolic of divine energy; and the index finger is symbolic of human energy. Therefore, if we want to feel more connected to the Divine, we try this mudra. Lastly, Anjali Mudra (hands in prayer) can be used to open and close a meditation or yoga class and it symbolizes an offering, balance, peace and harmony. Traditionally in a yoga class we set an intention at the beginning with our hands in Anjali Mudra. In my yoga-psychotherapy sessions, we end with Anjali Mudra and declare our intention for what we desire before we meet again. In my own meditations, I often start out by grounding with palms down. I switch midway to either receiving with palms facing up or to Gayan Mudra in order to feel a stronger connection to God and the universe. I close my meditation with Anjali Mudra and Namaste (the divine light in me honors the divine light in you) to God and the universe.

You may meditate just by focusing on the sound of the breath as we did with the Ujjayi breath in Chapter 10. Alternatively, you can stare at an object or something beautiful in nature with a soft gaze. When I do my meditations outside, I often meditate on the trees, flowers, a sunset or the ocean. For me, nature brings about an easier environment to clear my thoughts and meditate. For many of my clients, music can help bring them to a more peaceful, serene place. There is no right or wrong. You may sit or lie down to meditate, although if reclining, it may be harder not to fall asleep. This is why sitting is often recommended. I can better help an awake client than a sleeping one!

How to meditate is subjective, and only you can find the way that is most appropriate for you. I prefer for clients to begin small with just a few breaths at a time and gradually build up to five minutes per day, then ten minutes and eventually twenty to thirty minutes per day. Do not expect your thoughts to go away during meditation; that is not realistic. You will always have hundreds of thoughts. It is your relation to the thoughts that influences the outcome of the meditation. If you are having a thought that you cannot sit with, you can say to yourself, "This is an opportunity to practice letting it go." Over time, it becomes easier to connect and free your mind of all the thoughts. Sometimes it works and sometimes it does not. Nonetheless, the act of just sitting in stillness without noise can be liberating. As many times as it takes to come back to the present moment is okay.

Meditation can also be called "presence." Practicing internal and external "presence" offers immeasurable health benefits. My hope is for you to find a new way of being with "presence" in a consistent and open way.

Mindfulness

As mentioned in earlier Chapter 3, Jon Kabat-Zinn was important in popularizing in the West traditions and practices of meditation and mindfulness that originated in the East. He developed a program entitled *Mindfulness Based Stress Reduction* (MBSR) in 1979 in order to help chronically ill patients who were not responding to traditional therapeutic interventions. Today many hospitals, clinics and social service settings are sending their employees for the MBSR training.

Mindfulness is exactly what the name indicates. It is using your mind fully in order to pay attention and have awareness in the present moment. Mindfulness is not a quick fix and may take a lifetime to master. The topic has become mainstream and is popular in many magazines and articles nowadays. In fact, the 2016 special edition of

TIME magazine is entitled *Mindfulness, The New Science of Health and Happiness*. It is all about tuning into your body, the power of slow eating and mindfulness meditation. In addition to mindfulness now being mainstream, it has become an important part of many therapeutic models as people have become more open to and aware of the benefits of the body-mind connections.

In Dialectical Behavior Therapy (DBT), Marsha Linehan, founder and creator of the theory, adds the important element of mindfulness to Cognitive Behavioral Therapy (CBT). She initially used this to help teenagers with suicidal ideation (suicidal thoughts) but DBT is currently used for all ages and for numerous mental disorders. Linehan's work began the exploration of how being in the here-and-now can help troubled teens. In my practice, when I have clients with severe depression, tuning into the here-and-now and into their environment with full attention and awareness, provides some immediate relief, peace and comfort. Sometimes these positive feelings continue even after the session ends. The trick is to take the skills outside of the session and be able to do them on your own.

A simple mindfulness exercise you can try right now is to pick up an object that is near you. Once you have your object in hand, notice how it feels and notice its shape, size, texture, and its every angle and indentation.

Continue to feel your object and focus only on the object in hand, letting go of the rest of the world for the moment. Paying attention to your object is being mindful of the object. If you turn your attention instead towards your breath and focus on the breath alone, this is being "mindful" of the breath. The same can be done with feelings. No matter what the focus, mindfulness brings us back to the present moment and away from thoughts and worries about the past or future.

Mindfulness is a key component within my yoga practice. I teach a gentle Vinyasa yoga or yoga that flows in a mindful fashion as described earlier in Chapter 10. Once a position becomes uncomfortable, we quickly flow to the next position or posture. The emphasis is on the breath and the here-and-now.

In Kripalu yoga, there is an expression or acronym called BRFWA which stands for breathe, relax, feel, watch, and allow. With each letter of the acronym, the goal is to become more mindful. "Breathe" takes your attention to the breath. "Relax" engages the para-sympathetic nervous system, our rest and relax response. "Feel" takes you through a body scan noticing sensations in the body. "Watch" means witnessing your thoughts without getting attached to them. "Allow" is being in the present moment without judgment and accepting yourself for who you truly are.

You can try mindfulness exercises with almost anything you do, including brushing your teeth, chewing a piece of food, walking, running or just sitting. It requires slowing down and paying attention. Mindfulness deepens over time as you practice in each moment bringing yourself back to the present. The next time you are rushing, attempt to slow down and be mindful of what is causing you to rush. Taking the extra time to slow down may actually enhance your life in beautiful ways including your ability to connect with others. When we are truly present, others respond to us differently and the world becomes a more exciting, exuberant and peaceful place to be.

Meditation can be done mindfully, in the present moment, but this is not always the case. With mindfulness meditation your eyes are open or closed and you are completely in the here-and-now. Alternatively, transcendental meditation is mainly done with closed eyes and allows you to rise above the here-and-now, much like "going to the clouds." This practice actually takes you out of the present moment. The important distinction is whether you are working in the present moment or working to leave the present moment for a short time. Both are practices that can assist you in overcoming your worries or sadness and both have an enormity of current research on their psychological benefits.

Psycho-tips

- Meditation and mindfulness can be done anywhere at any time. They are not a quick fix; they are a way of life. Understand if your meditation is a mindfulness meditation or if you are rising above to a place that takes you beyond the here-and-now.
- You may start with ten deep breaths in the morning and ten deep breaths at night and try not to fall asleep.
- There is no right or wrong when it comes to meditation and mindfulness, just what res-onates with your being. If your mind wan-ders, bring it back to the present moment.
- There is ample research on brain changes from consistent meditation and mindfulness practice.
- Choose your favorite Mudra or hand position during meditation.
- Experiment with an object, becoming completely mindful of the object by feeling, observing and noticing every tiny detail about the object. You may try mindful brushing of your teeth or mindful eating.
- BRFWA—Breathe, Relax, Feel, Watch, Allow.

16

Animals and Mental Health

*"Me me me meeeeeeeeeeeowwwwwwwwwww,
purrrrrrrrrrrrrrrrrr, blrppppppppppp, WOOF!"*
–Snowflake, Red, Whiskey, and Salina

In 2008, I published an article in *Stamford Plus* Magazine entitled, *Soulmates; the Psychological Relationship Between Us and Our Pets and How They Keep Us Sane.* For a while the professional photo I used on *Psychology Today* was of me and my longtime, beautiful cat, Snowflake. Animals have immense healing properties by keeping us company and keeping us laughing. Laughter is one of the most beneficial coping mechanisms there is out there. My cat, Whiskey, also known as Mookey Latte, is the most vocal cat I know. He announces everything in the house with a very loud blurrpppttt. The sound he makes is not even describable, but it is hysterical and I hear it many times a day. He lets me know when he is going to eat, when he will take a drink, when he will move to a new place, when he will use the litter box, and so on. What a fabulous way to take the focus off of any stress or negativity and to bring me back to the present moment. Red, our other cat, is Daddy's little girl and I believe she keeps my husband, Chris, sane during his times of overwhelming stress. Growing up, Salina, my childhood dog, was my lifeline and my inspiration when there was a lot of fighting going on in the household. Lastly, Snowflake was my soulmate and she helped get me through 9/11.

Animals provided me much comfort during my post-9/11 experience. First and foremost, I offer a special thank you to the ASPCA and the police for the animal rescue they did in lower Manhattan after 9/11. They assisted me in rescuing Mini-me and Paisley, two adorable cats, who belonged to dear friends who could not get back to the neighborhood to care for them. The roads were all closed, so after rescuing them, I walked for miles to get uptown to provide them food and shelter. When we got to my apartment Mini-me bonded with my own cat, Snowflake, but neither one wanted anything to do with the smaller cat, Paisley. I slept that night in the tiny bathtub in my little studio apartment with Paisley, and we comforted each other. This was a mental health plus to sleep in the bathtub with the little one! These cats kept me sane during that very difficult time. It was the most challenging time in my life and I am so grateful that I was able to find my ground with the animals. People were scattered, communication with family was scarce, and my friends had all evacuated. In *Waking the Tiger, Healing Trauma,* Peter Levine talks about his car accident and how afterwards a human angel held his hand and let him know he would be all right. This touch was profound in helping him avoid suffering afterwards from Post-Traumatic Stress Disorder (PTSD). I believe Snowflake did the same for me, holding my hand for hours and days as I dealt with the aftermath of 9/11. The animals were the savior that day for many people's traumas and I am eternally grateful to have been part of rescuing them.

Psycho-tips

- If you have the time to lovingly care for a pet, they will care for you and help you through the most traumatic times.
- Find a way to laugh, because it is one of the most beneficial and beautiful coping mechanisms.
- Have an animal that will provide you with fun, joy and laughter.
- If it is not possible for you to have a pet, have a collection of funny videos that you can use to produce laughter during stressful times.
- Pet therapy is a proven way to decrease stress in times of sickness or crisis.
- Volunteering or helping out during a traumatic time can help you focus outward instead of on your mental turmoil.
- Reach out to your community during a crisis as people in crisis tend to bond together.

Taking The Edge Off:
Using Exercise To Improve Your Outlook

By Randall D. Martin, PhD, Licensed Psychologist

"Iron rusts from disuse, stagnant water loses its purity, and in cold weather becomes frozen; even so does inaction sap the vigors of the mind."
                                    –Leonardo da Vinci

I invited my colleague and confidant, Randy Martin, PhD, to write about the relationship between exercise and mental health. Dr. Martin is currently the Director of the Access Center at Humana's Employee Assistance Program in New York City. He is a licensed psychologist and HR/management consultant, has worked in numerous settings in both non-profit and corporate sectors, including employee assistance programs, mobile crisis teams, community mental health centers, developmental disability organizations, and crisis intervention services. Dr. Martin has been in the field more than 33 years. He has appeared on *WebMD, CNN Radio, 1010 WINS News Radio, WPIX Evening News*, and in web and print articles in, among others, *The Wall Street Journal's Market Watch,*

HR Executive Online, The Journal News, Time Out New York and *The National Herald.* He has expertise in the field of Positive Psychology, the scientific study of well-being and happiness, and has created and led numerous corporate seminars on the topic for clients like Citigroup, the Federal Reserve Bank of New York, and Columbia University. Dr. Martin earned his PhD in Psychology / Counseling from Indiana State University, a Master's in Counseling from the State University of New York at Albany, and a Bachelor of Arts degree from Wake Forest University.

In his own words is an account of how exercise can improve all aspects of your life:

"It was one of the most tense, stressful mornings of my life. In doctoral programs, after 3 years of graduate school classes, one must undergo the dreaded Comprehensive Exams. The "comps" (as they were called by students) comprised 3 days of grueling tests on everything one had studied in numerous courses over the past several years. It was a bear of a test, and I'd studied daily for hours, for several months, and now the moment was here: Time to face The Comps. What did I do that morning? I went for a 4-mile run. Sweating, considering the importance of the day, and mentally preparing for essentially an intellectual marathon, I pounded the pavement methodically on the sunny morning. When I finished, I felt calmer, more ready to face the day, more centered, and focused. I had taken the edge off my anxiety and worry by sweating some of it away. And it worked! I did well on the exams, and went on to become a licensed psychologist.

I'm no special elite athlete. I'm just a guy who has played various sports, some in school, but most casually with friends, and over time, came to feel that the sweating, the recovery, and often the camaraderie with others that happens when you do activities together, had a great impact on my ability to handle life's daily hassles, as well as its more significant challenges. I didn't need to study the impact of exercise on my mental health—I felt it in my bones. To me it just somehow made sense, that sweating seemed to exorcise the demons of sadness, softened disappointment, was a salve when I felt heartbroken, and helped me shake off tension when I was uptight or nervous. After a run, a bit of intensive weightlifting, hitting some tennis balls, or a vigorous walk, I just noticed I felt better. I felt ready. I felt in control. I developed more confidence, felt proud of myself, felt more empowered.

I studied psychology in college and decided to pursue becoming a therapist, as helping others using the science of psychology seemed like it would be gratifying and a good way to make my living. After I graduated from college and started graduate school, I noted how while we therapists-in-training were learning how to help our clients, we focused on helping them get in touch with their thoughts and feelings, examine the roots of them, look at family patterns, notice how we unknowingly recreate interactive patterns with people, and assist them in altering the way they think about themselves and situations using cognitive reframing. It was all fascinating and useful, but I kept thinking, 'What about how people's bodies impact the way they perceive things? What about the usefulness of helping people shape their minds not only by changing their thinking, but by helping them to see the critical importance of treating their body well, taking care of themselves physically? Could that help them feel better as well?'

Psychology from its inception in the early 1900's up until the 1980's was highly focused on the premise that our family and social environments shaped our personalities and helped us develop our most prevalent behavioral patterns. It was thought by most that Nurture (our environments, especially our family environments) was the prime driver and influence on our personality development.

In the 1990's and beyond, there has been a movement in the field that tied our biology (Nature) more to our personality development, based on twins studies and adoption studies that began to suggest that our biological makeup, our neurology, and the interaction between our environments and our bodies had a powerful influence on the development of our brains, and hence, our personalities. There was more of a focus on biological psychiatry, and the use of psychotropic (mind-changing) medicine and other medical/biological interventions (Transcranial Magnetic Stimulation, Vagus Nerve Stimulation, etc.) were touted as a more relevant solution (or at least one that should be paired with psychotherapy/talk therapy) to our psychological ills.

The pendulum had swung, from a focus on talk

therapy to biological interventions (chiefly medicine), so much so that many people seeking relief from psychological conditions now often go to their primary care physicians or other medical providers, and ask for and obtain medications, and medications only, for their problems. Due to a combination of conditions, including a national shortage of psychiatrists (medical doctors specially trained to treat psychiatric conditions), now consumers' primary care physicians (internists, family practice physicians, pediatricians) are prescribing 80 percent of all psychiatric medications. Sadly, these physicians often lack the training and resources that psychiatrists have, fail to offer thoughtful and thorough medication management and follow up care, and to me, most shockingly of all, often fail to recommend the pairing of medication-based treatment with psychotherapy and other useful adjunctive interventions, like exercise. This leads to people being placed on medications without providing them with additional tools of therapy, exercise, meditation, and mindfulness techniques.

I do not by any means have an anti-medication stance; there are times when medication is an essential component for people suffering from debilitating disorders like PTSD, anxiety, and depression (and many other disorders). But there are also many instances where medication might be avoided or minimized when psychotherapy, exercise, social support, and other interventions could be used in conjunction with it, or even instead of it. Medications have some downsides: they often cause undesirable side effects, can be costly, and can also make a person feel less empowered to help themselves, when they could be taking charge of their thoughts and their behaviors a bit more.

Exercise has few down sides when done properly, and is often no cost or low cost to put in place in one's life.

There is another benefit to exercise if you are a parent or a caretaker of another person, like a developmentally disabled sibling or an older parent or relative: Modeling. According to Dr. Jordan Metzl from the Hospital for Special Surgery in New York City, all of us are in the midst of an "inactivity epidemic" that is damaging our health in countless ways. When we take care of our bodies through exercise, we model for our children and our family members a behavior that will give them lifelong tools to prevent or minimize physical and mental ills. They watch what we do, and may emulate us. So by helping yourself in this way, you are also teaching others an important coping mechanism.

It seems that many professionals and academicians in the social sciences field have also been noticing how perhaps therapists and researchers should take a closer look at the exercise-mental health connection. The American Psychological Association says " . . . as the evidence piles up, the exercise-mental health connection is becoming impossible to ignore."

The September 2016 cover story of *TIME* magazine is titled "The Exercise Cure." In it, researchers note the numerous physiological and psychological benefits of exercise, and it's clear that finally, the benefits of fitness have become clear to all manner of medical and psychological healing arts professionals. Dr. Mark Tarnopolsky, a researcher at McMaster University in Ontario says: " . . . paper after paper shows that the most effective, potent way we can improve quality of life and duration of life is exercise." The writer notes that "If there were a drug that could do for human health everything that exercise can, it would likely be the most valuable pharmaceutical ever developed."

Here is the problem: only 20% of Americans get the recommended 150 minutes of strength and cardiovascular exercise per week. Of that 20% who do exercise, many do not do both cardiovascular and weight-bearing exercise. What I've observed is that often women only focus on cardio (running, walking, Stairmaster, elliptical, etc.), and often men focus on anaerobic strength training like weightlifting. The very best exercise regimens include a mix of both, as they offer different and important benefits.

What does exercise do for us physiologically?

- Slows the aging process
- Invigorates sexual functioning
- Improves sleep quality
- Decreases chronic pain
- Improves energy level, and endurance
- Reduces cholesterol
- Improves cardiovascular functioning
- Improves vision
- Increases body temperature, which may have calming effects

- Reduces immune system chemicals that can worsen depression
- Improves blood flow to the brain, feeding the growth of new blood vessels and brain cells
- May slow down the aging of cells
- Lowers risk of cancer, diabetes, stroke, and early death
- Reduces inflammation, an increasing focus of researchers as a cause of many ills
- Increases brain chemicals that improve mood (endorphins, dopamine, norepinephrine, serotonin and endocannabinoids)
- Relaxes muscles, relieving tension

What does exercise do for us cognitively?

- Improves memory
- Promotes quicker learning
- Improves concentration
- Improves motivation

What does exercise do for us psychologically and emotionally?

- Improves mood (usually within 5 minutes of moderate exercise)
- Decreases anxiety, worry, and stress
- Lowers depression
- Increases self-confidence, self-esteem and provides a sense of accomplishment

- Improves self-efficacy, the belief that we can succeed at things
- Helps us develop friendships with people with whom we exercise, obtaining and giving social support
- Improves resilience from daily hassles and stressors
- Generates a feeling of well-being and calmness/serenity
- Provides a healthy distraction from our daily worries

On Depression, Anxiety, ADHD, and Trauma

Regular, sustained exercise can minimize and reduce symptoms of depression, anxiety/worry, Attention Deficit Hyperactivity Disorder (ADHD), and Post-Traumatic Stress Disorder (PTSD). Some cool things about exercise:

- There are no co-pays at the pharmacy; there are no side effects from medications; and it can be a life-long habit.
- The distraction that exercise can provide, the single minded focus of returning a tennis serve, or focusing on a yoga position, can take your mind off worries about what happened at work yesterday or the bills you have to pay tonight. It allows us to be 'in the moment' and achieve mindfulness.
- The friendly connection you make with people in your spinning class, or your walking partner, can

be very supportive. It also offers you a chance to support others, which is another aspect of contentment we often forget, and which provides us with many positive feelings.

- Exercise can help prevent relapse. It gives you healthy alternatives to drinking too much, drugging, overeating, and other compulsive behaviors like shopping, gaming, gambling, and excessive sexual behaviors.
- Exercise is generally comparable to antidepressants for patients with major depressive disorder, and is also helpful in preventing relapse.
- Exercise can help ward off panic attacks.
- Exercise may be a way of biologically toughening up the brain so stress has less of an impact.

What should you do to improve your physical and mental health?

- Build exercise into your daily routine, make it a part of almost every day.
  - It may help (it helps me) to do it as soon as you wake up, or after your first cup of coffee/tea. The timing of early morning exercise means that 1) nothing gets in your way and gives you an excuse to skip it, and 2) exercise at the start of the day provides what psychologists call 'stress inoculation.' It's like a booster shot to help you deal with the daily hassles and stressful events we all face every day.

- Exercise for 30 minutes, 5 times per week (150 minutes total).
- You can break the 30 minutes up into 3 10-minute workouts, or 2 15-minute workouts, if that helps.
- Mix cardiovascular activities (walking, running, swimming, biking, Stairmaster/elliptical) with strength training (weight training, yoga, Tai Chi, Pilates, push-ups, pull-ups, etc.).
- Remember that activities that involve movement are a form of exercise! Things like gardening, housework, and even standing lead to lower levels of stress and anxiety.
- Take the stairs instead of the escalator or elevator.
- Walk instead of drive when possible.
- Get off the bus, subway or train 1 or 2 stops early and walk.

Tackling the Barriers: How to Prevent Excuses Not to Exercise:

- **I don't have time:** Do High Intensity Interval Training (HIIT)—New research shows that working out at a high intensity, but short duration (e.g., 10–30 minutes) can be just as good for you as 60 minutes at moderate intensity. If you are time crunched due to professional or personal responsibilities, ramp up your intensity.
- **I'm not motivated**: Partner with a friend for companionship, motivation, and accountability; they

will help you 'just do it' when you are tempted to skip it.

- **I'm too tired or drained**: Remind yourself that a bit of movement will help renew and refresh you. Oddly, exercise gives you more energy, trust me!
- **I'm overwhelmed by the thought of adding exercise**: Start small and build from there, even if it's 10 minutes a day, most days per week; best to add structure.
- **I don't want to be in pain**: All that's needed is moderate levels of exercise, where you breathe a little heavier than normal, but don't get out of breath, and that your body feels warmer as you move, but not very sweaty. In time, you may embrace pushing yourself a bit harder.

A few caveats:

- Don't rely solely on exercise for weight loss or weight maintenance as you grow older.
  - Exercise sometimes increases weight due to increased muscle mass and heartier appetite.
  - Focus on portion control and healthy eating in addition; just a few weeks on Weight Watchers, using their mobile app, for example, can teach you what a reasonable portion size is, and what foods to minimize and maximize.

It's very clear that incorporating regular, aerobic and strength-building exercise will have a global impact on your body and your mind. The very best way to start is using structure, regularity, and where possible, a social connection with others to get you up and moving, and keep you motivated. In a very short time, you will no doubt notice how exercise improves your mood, and takes the edge off the stressful parts of your day."

Randy's Psycho-tips

- Find fun things to do that are active, like playing Frisbee with your kids.
- Mix up your routine: Don't do the same exercise each day, keep trying new things to keep it fresh and interesting (even dancing is exercise and according to Pamela, it's better exercise than anything else because you utilize every muscle in your body, mind and soul).
- If you are not doing weight bearing exercise, add it (weightlifting, SoulCycle, yoga, Pilates, push-ups, pull-ups, etc.).
- Structure, structure, structure: "I exercise every weekday," "I exercise Mon/Wed/Fri," "I exercise alternate days" —it builds in a habit that you simply get used to, which makes doing it easier.
- Don't get caught up in long exercise routines if you are short on time: Do high intensity, short-burst, vigorous workouts for 15–30 minutes on days when time is crunched, and do longer workouts on weekends, for example.

- Treat yourself to some nice looking athletic wear to look and feel your best.
- Invest in yourself: Add that gym membership, buy that stationary bike, or join those yoga or CrossFit classes or purchase personal training sessions for yourself. Find friends or coworkers to join you, adding a social component to your routine. You deserve it!

Part Four

Nourishing Your Soul: Overcoming Trauma

Saucha: Treating Your Body As a Temple

"The body is your temple. Keep it pure and clean for the soul to reside in."
                                              —BKS Iyenger

Nourishment, cleanliness and purity come to mind when I think of the yoga teaching of Saucha (shou-cha). Saucha is one of the *Niyamas* (personal observances) in yoga as listed in Chapter 11. Saucha simply means treating your body as a temple or "purity."

If you think of your body as holy, you will treat it with loving care. Cleaning the clutter out of your mind and body is like a detox of the heart. Once you take impeccable care of your body, your heart will fill with self-love, your mind will become more open and clear and you will look fantastic!

How do we care for our bodies as if they are sacred?

- Eat nourishing whole foods, without pesticides or additives.

- Eat organic food, and if this is not possible, then wash your fruits and vegetables thoroughly with soap or a vegetable wash.

- Take time to be mindful and slow down.

- Take time to prepare food ahead of time instead of grabbing "whatever" at the last minute.

- Be kinder to your body.

- Eat a colorful array of fruits and vegetables in order to provide important anti-oxidants in addition to hydrating your muscles, tissues and organs.

- Slow down your chewing time to savor each bite.

- Avoid saturated fat to help you clean your arteries and keep yourself lean.

- Choose fish instead of meat a few times a week to help provide healthy oils that will rejuvenate your joints and diminish inflammation. Freshwater or wild caught are recommended.

- Avoid foods that may cause allergens such as white bread and white flour.

- Avoid sugar whenever possible and use natural sources of sweeteners like stevia, agave or honey.

Healthy choices in food CAN be delicious. Once you are choosing more fruits and vegetables, you will be able to eat a larger quantity and feel less full. The full feeling after eating a large bowl of pasta is what we are trying to avoid when we speak of Saucha. Eat what you love and only the amount that you need. When I work with Binge Eating Disorder clients in my practice, people complain that they are hungry at night. A cup of herbal tea can do wonders for the stomach and for your mood. Also, if you do not eat to excess, you will get used to the smaller amounts and will not need as much food to be satisfied in the future.

There are many qualified nutritionists and registered dieticians who can help you with this. I work with the behavioral aspect that causes people to eat in excess. The first step is to pay attention to this behavior, notice your thoughts and feelings when you are eating unhealthy foods, note them on paper in a food journal, and recognize any repetitive patterns of emotional eating. Once you bring awareness to this, you can begin treating your body as the beautiful sanctuary that it is. Writing down your feelings and thoughts when you have a food trigger is a Cognitive Behavioral Therapy (CBT) technique. This can be helpful in monitoring your intake of unhealthy foods and recognizing the emotions you are feeling when you do reach for them.

Cleanliness is also associated with Saucha. During a major depression, one of the things people tend to avoid is being as clean as they can be. What they do not realize is that just the act of showering or bathing and having the water on their skin can help lift them out of the lows and bring them back to equilibrium. However, it is not easy to do this when you are so depressed that you cannot even get out of bed. Think of the shower or bath water as a cleansing, a purification; the more we purify ourselves, the more likely we are to feel better about ourselves. It is also helpful to have a clean body and a clean space during prayer and meditation. Eliminating clutter from your space will assist you in feeling better about yourself. Practicing impeccable self-care along with acting with honesty and integrity is an excellent way to clean up your life.

Respecting your body will allow your body to respect you by being healthy and alive. Over time you can have a new appreciation for your body with all the self-care that comes with Saucha.

Psycho-tips

- Treat your body with loving care and keep it clean.
- Nourish your body with whole foods and healthy foods and slow down your chewing time.
- Eat colorful fruits and vegetables every day; in addition to nutrition they provide hydration.
- Avoid white bread and white flour because of the allergens.
- Take time to prepare food ahead of time instead of grabbing "whatever" at the last minute.
- Clean the clutter in your sacred space in order to clean the clutter in your body, mind and spirit.
- Eat fish a few times a week for anti-inflammation.

19

The Value of Friendship

*"God has been unkind to me for having me born
so long ago that I can't court you!"*
—Ange Gardien

There is nothing like friendship, companionship, acceptance, support and love. People who see us in our truest "light" give us permission to be our authentic selves, reveal our secrets and share our deepest fears and pain. I was lucky enough to have a special friend like this, in fact, a best friend. I call him Ange Gardien (guardian angel) and I am sad to say he is no longer with us. With Ange Gardien I revealed my past mistakes, my inner shame and was accepted for who I was. He was an older man whom I loved unconditionally and who loved me in return. The relationship was purely platonic and one of great respect. He was a physician and a researcher, and we shared many special memories.

I met Gardien when I was living in Los Angeles after I graduated from my undergraduate studies. We had a wonderful time together exploring the city and traveling abroad. My most memorable moment with him was dancing at the Lido in Paris before the show began. The band was playing and we cleared the dance floor. Of course, there were people who assumed we were a couple and were horrified by the age difference. However, there was nothing romantic about this relationship. We just had pure love and mutual respect. We accepted each other with all our faults. I pray for everyone in the world to experience this form of love.

Gardien was known for his funny, flirtatious lines which were repetitive and silly. He would always say them to the young girls he met; and he got away with it, because he was so much older and was so loving and non-threatening. He stopped every pretty girl we passed on the streets of L.A. and he would say, *"God has been unkind to me for having me born so long ago that I can't court you!"* This was one of his favorites, and he always got a smile. He thrived on this! I once figured out that over the 18 years that I knew him I heard this line 6,552 times! It was endearing, because when he said the line to me he really meant it. If he had been born 40 years later, we may have been a couple.

Gardien loved me for the good, the bad and the ugly. It was pure unconditional love. Mostly we receive this type of acceptance and love from pets. As far as human relationships go, they always come and go with a set of expectations. Even the most enlightened of beings may have trouble with interpersonal relationships. Families also have multiple difficulties with unconditional love. All of our issues surface when we are with our immediate families. One of my teachers once said, "If you want to test how enlightened you are, go home to your mom or mother-in-law."

This is the reason my relationship with Gardien was so special. He could tell me anything; and I could tell him anything no matter how much shame I had about it. Whatever secret I shared was always received with humor and tenderness. Many clients come to me with an enormous amount of guilt and shame from things they have done over their lifetimes. People hold onto things about themselves that they are not proud of. This can produce an enormity of self-loathing. As their therapist, one of the most difficult jobs for me is to assist them in seeing that they are not terrible people because they made a mistake at some point in their lives. Self-forgiveness is an even harder task than forgiving others. It has to come with self-love and self-care that we spoke of earlier.

If you do not have a dear friend who loves you unconditionally who can help you with self-love, imagine yourself as a child seeing the world through innocent eyes. If a child, whether it be your offspring or your own inner child, made a huge mistake would you forgive that child? I know that I would. Parents will love and protect their children even if one of them is a bully on the playground, has taken drugs, has stolen, has lied, has cheated, or has beaten someone up. Forgiveness is liberating and can not only free you from heartache, it can also have a profound effect on the person who is being forgiven. It can have so much power that it can lead to a radical transformation in both the forgiven person and in the person doing the forgiving. Forgiveness is empowering. You can release all guilt and shame and hand it to the universe, God, a higher power or whatever entity feels right to you. You deserve to live your life to the fullest, to love and honor yourself, to be kind to yourself and to forgive yourself.

Self-forgiveness is the path to freedom. I openly admit that as a teenager I lied and I was selfish. Even in my earlier years I would start fights on the playground. My mom always reminds me about the time a neighbor came over to tell her that I bit her daughter's ear. I do not remember this! I must have been five or six years old. Thankfully, I am not that person today and I have apologized and made amends to those who I have hurt. If I could change the past I would. I was in emotional pain back then, and I did the best I could. My home was in turmoil, and my parents constantly argued as their marriage came to an end. I have forgiven everyone for their behavior including myself, which is most important but often the most difficult thing to do. Also, recently just before one of my teenage buddies passed away (may she rest in peace), she expressed her forgiveness to me for something hurtful I did over thirty years ago. I will be eternally grateful to her for that acknowledgement.

An example of forgiveness and radical transformation can be seen in the Broadway musical, *Les Misérables*. Jean Valjean is imprisoned for stealing a loaf of bread. After Valjean escapes prison, he steals silver from a bishop who had been kind to him and had provided food and shelter when he was homeless and hungry. When Valjean gets caught by the police, the bishop pardons and forgives him, and tells the police that he had given the silver to Valjean as a gift. This begins Jean Valjean's journey and transformation toward becoming a better man. The Bishop sings to him about the meaning of the silver and how he must use it to become an honest man. Even though I have seen the musical ten times, the song (second one on the soundtrack) still brings chills to my spine. Song number three on the soundtrack fully shows Valjean's transformation. The song is about Valjean's shame and how he will now release his shame to the universe and God. It touches my soul every time because it was my journey too. The melodies are extraordinary in addition to the meaning.

My hope for you is that you begin a practice of forgiveness and that you have true friends who can help you with this. If forgiveness does not seem attainable for you, then acceptance (Chapter 25) will provide a pathway towards physical, emotional and spiritual healing.

Psycho-tips

- Understand and be mindful of the people in your life who love you for whom you truly are.
- Apologize to those you have hurt and make amends.
- Do not expect forgiveness in return; just move on.
- Release your inner shame and forgive yourself for anything you have done that causes you to feel guilt, regret or sadness. Learn a valuable lesson from it in order to not repeat the upsetting behavior again.
- Understand that your parents did the best they could, given their emotional state.
- Treat yourself with the love you would give a child.
- If an act is unforgivable, release it to the universe or God so that you can begin to move forward in your life.

20

Aging Gracefully

"As one gets older, exercising your brain as well as your body is extremely beneficial. Staying involved in the community through volunteering is another great way to exercise your mind and body."

—Nadine R. Benoit, MPA

In my yoga classes whenever we go into Downward Facing Dog, an inverted position where our head is below our heart, I tell everyone that this is an easy way to get a face lift. The blood flowing to the face allows for more circulation; it will add beauty and take away years of hardship from the face. My yogis are probably tired of hearing me say this. Research indicates that yoga can keep you youthful, vibrant, radiant, flexible and full of young energy. There is nothing like going upside down to change your energy and perspective. During my yoga training, the first time I was assisted in doing a handstand I understood this completely. My instructor at the time said to me, "Once you go upside down, you will never want to be right side up." However, I do not recommend trying a handstand without the appropriate training because as your shoulders age, they are not as flexible and major tears can happen quite easily.

There is something that happens when we see the world from upside down. It is like putting on a different pair of glasses. In *A Course In Miracles*, which Dave Asomaning, PhD speaks about in Chapter 27, there is the concept of illusion versus truth. The premise is that what we see in front of us is an illusion that our minds make up and consequently we create our own world view and our own destiny. This means that we create our own dramas and our own peace. Taking a look at the world through a different lens will allow us to gain a larger perspective and be open-minded to an alternative way of seeing things. In Buddhist beliefs the "illusion" is called a "delusion." For example, if you did not know your age, the answer to how old you are would be one of illusion and perception. This goes back to seeing the world upside down. It is a shift in focus and perception that can allow us to gain clarity from a new angle. As we see things upside down we may start to view things more positively when we are right side up.

Aging gracefully is something we all strive for, and hopefully after reading the chapters about self-care, self-worth, fitness, mental health, and how to heal your traumas, you can begin to see that taking care of yourself is a key component in aging gracefully. Impeccable self-care will lead you to your golden years with a sense of accomplishment, clarity and grace. As stated in the quote earlier from Nadine Benoit, MPA, Coordinator of the Hospital Elder Life Program at Hackensack University

Medical Center, keeping the mind active also plays a huge role in quality of life.

According to Benoit, remaining active in your community and maintaining long-term friendships will be beneficial in your later years, and will even help with issues of depression, loneliness, and anxiety. It is common for older people to become depressed when they lose a spouse and become isolated. Being a part of a community is essential to your well-being, whether it is at a community center, temple, church or another organization.

Activities play a huge role in maintaining physical and mental health as one grows older. Keeping a schedule of events, even if you are wheelchair bound, will enable you to feel productive and have something to look forward to daily. Even if your activity is just having someone take you outside daily, this will brighten your mood and enhance your abilities to cope with the isolation that can come with aging and being non-mobile.

Lastly, reaching out to those in need will help you take the focus off of your own loneliness and give you the purpose of helping others. When we focus on helping others, our own issues and traumas seem to lesson as we realize how fortunate we are to be able to assist others with their dilemmas.

Psycho-tips

- You will age gracefully with yoga, even if you are just doing Pranayama (breathing exercises) daily. If you are able to do *Downward Facing Dog*, you may have a natural face lift from extra blood flow.
- Reach out to community, friends and family when you feel isolated.
- Have a schedule of daily activities to continue to have purpose.
- See the world through a different lens, an upside down one.
- Take impeccable care of yourself.
- Go outside every day.
- Help those in need in order to focus outward, thereby healing your own issues and traumas also.

21

YogaDance

"To dance is to be out of yourself; larger, more beautiful, more powerful. This is power, it is glory on earth and it is yours for the taking."
—Agnes de Mille

My best work to date with teaching YogaDance was done at the Greenwich Senior Center in Greenwich, Connecticut, from 2012 to 2014. There are many forms of YogaDance; and most of them are done with feeling, passion and free style movements. The class I created had simple choreography and was based on basic ballet and jazz dance principles. It added the spiritual elements, the meditative aspects, and some of the postures of yoga along with a dance motif.

The most inspiring aspect of teaching this class was to see the enthusiasm and appreciation of the students. Some of the students were in their nineties, and they had more energy and passion than many people I know in my own age group. They were fortunate enough to be able to move around; and although many had aches and pains, they would tell me that the hour that I was there was the best time of their week. They thoroughly enjoyed the music I played which was a combination of oldies and modern music. To my surprise, they often knew all the words to even the newer songs.

The seniors were eager to learn and brave enough to dance one at a time in the middle of the circle we created to "show off" their moves. I learned quickly that when you age, you become less self-conscious and just enjoy yourself without worrying about what people think. When I teach the class to younger students, there is always a great amount of trepidation. The seniors exhibited not only an absence of fear, but great passion, joy and creative expression.

Dance is uplifting and can be spiritual and grounding at the same time. It combines the energy of the universe with the joy of bodily sensations and the sense of being in your body, grounded, rooted and connected to the earth. Even if you do not like to dance, try it alone in your living room with music that you love. Just bopping to the beat can have significant positive effects on your state of being. If you are older and bound to a wheelchair or walker, maybe you can still move your hands and feel the rhythm of the music. Even micro-dance movements can create joy, a sense of youth and a playful nature. As stated in Chapter 17, in my opinion dance is the best workout you can do for your body, mind and soul. Try it sometime! You might surprise yourself if you have not embraced it before.

Psycho-tips

- YogaDance is a beautiful healing modality.
- As you age, dancing can keep you youthful and healthy.
- To dance is to connect to spiritual aspects and physical grounding.
- Yoga and dance can bring you energy and passion. The combination is invigorating.
- As you age you will possibly become less self-conscious.
- Aging may bring you wisdom and creative freedom.
- Try dancing in your living room to your favorite music even if you think you cannot dance.

22

Mantras

"I learned it all in AA."
–Anonymous

As mentioned in previous chapters, a mantra is a repeated word or phrase that we say to ourselves to help remain positive. It is a positive affirmation that is repeated numerous times a day.

There are many mantras I recommend, however, it is always best to create your own, something that resonates with your spirit. What has worked well for my clients and me is to have alerts on our phones that pop up and remind us of our affirmations or mantras. I have three or four morning alerts and a few in the evening as well. I am always delighted and surprised when they appear, even though my phone has been programmed like that for a while.

In many yoga programs, the mantras begin with "I am" such as "I am healthy" or "I am lovable." However, when we say "I am," our psyches sometimes react and fight back and say "No, I'm not!," especially if there is a tendency towards negative thinking. If this is the case, I recommend taking out the "I am" and just using one word such as "health" or "love." This will allow the mantra to register into your being without the resistance.

Below are some of the mantras I use and some from other professionals as well. The first mantra listed, *"Samastitihi* (sa-mas-ti-ti-hi) . . . *I love me,"* can be done after a sun salutation (gratitude to the sun) in yoga where you bring your hands first to prayer for equal balance and then touch your heart to bring in self-love (adapted from Mariana Caplan, PhD):

"Samastitihi . . . I love me!"

"God and I manifest an abundance of miracles into my life now."

"I release all guilt and shame."

"May the heat of hatred turn into the love of forgiveness."

"I turn fear into love."

"I am beautiful / handsome."

"I am a Warrior Goddess!"

"I am a Jewish Warrior Princess."

"I am powerful."

"I am free."

"I am worthy."

"God is always with me."

"I trust." or just *"trust"*

"I am lovable." or just *"lovable"*

"I shine."

"I can rise above this."

"I am health." or just *"health"*

"Thank you for this amazing opportunity."

"I love you."

"I am grateful."

"I accept myself."

"The light always wins."

"I only invite love, light and God."

"Inhale love . . . exhale fear."

"I am with you."
—Jennifer S. Greer, Certified Coach and RYT® 500

"Magical things happen outside of my comfort zone."
—Amanda Jablon, ACSW

"I am here now."
—Vincent Fraser, CST, CAT

*"I learn through real love, joy and bliss in
my relationship."*
—Anthony Vatuna

"God is the light in which I trust."
—A Course In Miracles

"What you seek is seeking you."
*"The wound is the place where
the light enters you."*
—Rumi

*"The world is a more colorful place when
I have self-compassion."*
—Daniel Rosenstein

"Kol Ha-neshamah T'hallel Yah."
(kol-ha-ne-sha-ma-tal-lel-yah) defined as:
"Every Breath Celebrates the Source of Life."
—Leonard Felder, PhD

"I have all the time I need to be present
in this moment."
"Going towards what scares me
is the way to mastery."
—Sandra Eagle, LCSW

"Whatever it is, let it go. You have the
whole world in front of you."
—Jacqueline Day, RYT®

"Challenge your body. Empower your life!"
—Angela Hubbs

"Come to me now, I am the beacon.
I am exactly what you have been seeking."
—Liz Ross

"Notice the blue sky. Feel the warmth
of the sunshine."
—Joyce Gerber

"Family is always there."
—The Benoit Family

There are many more and you can be creative with your mantras, affirmations and phone alerts so that you are reminded of positive thoughts and feelings daily.

The following mantra was said by me during a session with a client who has a severe and dangerous eating disorder:

"You can go into cardiac arrest in a heartbeat."

The above comment was unplanned and, while we had a good laugh, it is not a joking matter.

Although the mantra is not a positive affirmation, it has caused the client to be more mindful about healthy eating.

"May you find your MOJO!"

Psycho-tips

- Have a mantra or mantras that you repeat many times throughout the day.
- Create ones that resonate with your being and that do not cause you to react and fight back.
- Your mantra can be one word or a phrase.
- Create alerts on your phone that pop up throughout the day as a reminder to slow down and say your mantra. (This is my favorite tool.)
- Practice breathing deeply, as you repeat your mantra.
- Inhale your mantra and on the exhale send it out to the universe.
- Breathe the mantra into your being, make it an intention, and extend your arms outward with palms facing upward, ready to receive.

23

Surrender

with Cantor Magda Fishman

"Something amazing happens when we surrender and just love. We melt into another world, a realm of power already within us. The world changes when we change. The world softens when we soften. The world loves us when we choose to love the world."
—Marianne Williamson

When we speak of "surrender," we are not referring to a game or even a battlefield where you wave a white flag to let the enemy know that you are defeated. Surrender in spiritual terms is not associated with defeat. In fact, it is quite the opposite. When we surrender to the universe or the Divine, we give up the need to control everything in our lives and we actually let go. We allow something far greater than ourselves to take over.

For many clients, turning towards a power greater than themselves can help provide reassurance that things will work out. Prayer is similar to surrender and both can be used when dealing with psychological and physical trauma. I primarily work with psychological trauma which in most cases affects a person's physical well-being. The trauma becomes stored in the anatomy and cannot be released unless the body-mind process has begun.

Surrender and prayer can work together on trauma to help take the focus off "I" and onto a larger perspective of healing with assistance from the universe or God. It is not an alternative to doing the much needed somatic work for trauma. It is in addition to the therapeutic work and can be helpful to broaden one's view and increase one's hope.

I invited *Cantor Magda Fishman* from Temple Beth El in Stamford, Connecticut to reflect on prayer as we ponder the possibilities of being assisted by a power greater than ourselves:

In the Cantor's words:

"Praying for me is meditation of the heart, body and soul.

It's a connection to the universe, to my body and soul and to the people around me.

It's an energy that connects people to people, people to the world and people to God. (I refer to God as our creator but there are other names for this divine energy.)

It's the time that I disconnect from the noises and everything around me and re-connect with everything in a different way—in a slower, more conscious way that allows me to stop running.

I stop, and by giving my soul through prayer, I gain energy and peace of mind. The interesting part is that as a leader of prayer, I am exhausted afterwards, but at the same time I am also uplifted.

Prayer can be in silence with our soul praying without words or it can be done with words: the words of our ancestors, words of our heart, words of poetry and words of love.

Whatever makes your soul connect to the universe, to yourself and to others is a song of prayer for me."

In my office I have what is called a God box. If you do not believe in God, you can instead have a universe box or a prayer box. It is a little wooden box that I use when I face a situation that I cannot resolve. The origins of the God box are unknown. However, I learned about it from a friend who states that everything he knows is from his Alcoholics Anonymous (AA) experience. Somewhere in the rooms of AA this idea may have once developed or possibly it came from a church setting long before AA's existence.

When you are having a situation that is gripping you where you cannot let go, and when thoughts are occupying your every moment, it can be helpful to write about it on a small piece of paper and put the paper in a God box. Forget about the situation and allow the universe or God to take care of it for you. I go through my God box about every three months and to my amazement, most of the things I was so consumed with are no longer issues. I also have a box which was a beautiful gift and on the outside cover is says, "Prayer Box." On the inside cover it says, *"When your head starts to worry, and your mind just can't rest, put your prayers down on paper, and let God do the rest."* Your God or prayer box does not have to be anything fancy. It can be a jewelry box, a cardboard box or any container that you can keep in a private place. Many times we do not want to write about things that someone in our household could potentially find. If that is the case, just write "code" or initials. God knows what you are referring to!

You Are Enough

When you are feeling low
And cannot let go
Surrender to God
And the rest will flow

If you cannot go on
And think love is gone
Be yourself and be free
Love passionately

Relax and be wise
Choose when to compromise
Be skillful and aware
Always take good care

Put fear to the test
Let your essence be your best
Shine so bright
Shine your brightest light

For now, give a hug
When your heart feels a tug
Don't lose faith, it will change
Your life will re-arrange

Love yourself and be free
Trust yourself completely
Open and care
For those you love, who will always be there

Take time for YOU
Only you can break through
It is your time to soar
Let life hear you roar!

Psycho-tips

- When you are overwhelmed, surrender and release your worries to the universe or God.
- Have a God box, universe box or prayer box where you can write your worries down on a piece of paper and hand them over to be solved by a power greater than yourself.
- Go through this box every three months or sooner to see what issues have been resolved and remove them.
- Surrender does not mean "defeat;" it means "trust" in spiritual terms.
- An AA saying is "Let go, let God."
- "Surrender and just love."
- If you are feeling down, you can read the poem, *You Are Enough.*

24

Embracing Change

"Change may be frightening,
but also frightening is NO CHANGE."
　　　　　　　　　　　–Karin Gerber

There's an adorable little book that I have recommended to so many clients over the years. It is entitled *Who Moved My Cheese,* by Spencer Johnson, MD. You can read it in about a half hour and learn a lifetime's worth of lessons. I will not reveal the story. I will tell you that you will be able to identify with one of the characters in the book and will see what happens when he is faced with the uncomfortable. One of the lines in the book is that *if you do not change you can become extinct.* If you think about that for a moment it rings true. We must change in order to grow and expand. We, as humans, can become overly comfortable and complacent and when it is time to change, we often resist and revert back to our old routines and our old ways. What is it about change that we often resist? In my office I have a plaque that says, "If nothing ever changed, there'd be no butterflies." (There is also a humorous plaque that says, "Who needs therapy when you have wine?"). Part of the human condition is that we are fearful of change. When we are asked to stretch outside of our comfort zone, we often freeze to some extent. This does not apply to everyone and I am overgeneralizing. However, most people who enter therapy are having some difficulties with transitions in their lives.

To embrace change means to open yourself willingly. How do you open when your body is closing down? The words trust and faith come to mind. The times when we need to trust and have faith are often the times when we lack it. Change comes more effortlessly when things are going our way. We can become angry at the universe or God when times get rough. It is sort of like a pity party when we do not have our way and life is not moving in a positive direction. We may say, "Woe is me, poor me, why me, these are the cards I was dealt," instead of saying, "I'm going to keep swimming" (like Nemo says in *Finding Nemo*, "*Just keep swimming!*"). Of course, it is much more difficult to "keep swimming" when we are going through a traumatic event. This is when we have to dig down even deeper to our internal resources for support and strength.

When we are faced with difficult situations that require us to shift and change, we are at the edge of our comfort zone. At these moments we are being asked to stretch outside of ourselves. Connecting to our insides at these moments will allow us to notice where our edges are and to see if we can tolerate going outside the edges very slowly. The problem with trauma is that it can be sudden and we do not have time to slow it down in the moment. Our nervous system goes into shock and it is difficult to settle it down. Stabilization becomes possible when we learn and practice the appropriate tools for healing.

Change comes easily to few people. Even if it seems effortless in other's lives, remember that you are seeing their outsides, not their insides. We all have challenges when we need to "stretch" and we all have some form of resistance that comes about. You can try to notice the resistance without judgment and move forward anyway, even though you may be scared. Courage takes confidence and confidence takes time to develop. Be patient with the process and embrace change!

Psycho-tips

- Notice how much you resist change.
- Try to open willingly with trust and faith (easier said than done).
- Avoid victim statements such as "woe is me" or "poor me."
- After a traumatic event try to slow things down in order to reorient. Trauma will shock your nervous system and force change abruptly. Remember to breathe deeply to allow the change to permeate.
- Stretch outside of your comfort zone very slowly and explore your edges.
- Resistance is a normal reaction to change.
- Be patient with yourself and "embrace change."

25

Acceptance

"Acceptance is the answer to all my problems today. When I am disturbed, it is because I find some person, place, thing or situation—some fact of my life—unacceptable to me, and I can find no serenity until I accept that person, place, thing or situation as being exactly the way it is supposed to be at this moment. Unless I accept life on life's terms, I cannot be happy. I need to concentrate not so much on what needs to be changed in the world as on what needs to be changed in me and my attitudes."
                        –Alcoholics Anonymous

What are we actually accepting? Are we accepting ourselves for better or worse? Accepting our neighbors? Accepting our families? That is a tough one. We can be the most enlightened of beings until we come home to our parents (if we are lucky enough to still have them). It is amazing that once we are with our parents, we revert back to feeling like a child. Even if our parents are elderly and at this point in life we have more strength, wisdom and knowledge to offer than they do, they may not willingly relinquish their parental authority.

Acceptance is not an easy task and if we were all good at it, there would be no conflict, no stress, no worry and no doubt. Acceptance is particularly hard for people who have been a victim of a crime. They will not accept their perpetrator's behavior and this is entirely understandable. No one is asking the victim to forgive. It is not about accepting the criminal behavior as anything but heinous. In order to move on, however, the victim must accept that the traumatic event happened, that it is in the past and that there is no way to change it. Moving on from traumatic events can be difficult and almost impossible in some cases. Moving on does not mean leaving it behind completely; the event will always be with us. It suggests, however, that we move forward and continue on while still carrying some of the memory with us.

Welcoming people for who they are with a non-judgmental stance is another form of acceptance. This can be difficult especially when people mirror our own issues, the parts of ourselves we do not like, and negative emotions are triggered. Did you ever hate someone without even knowing them? Sometimes this happens and six months later you find out that person is amazing! You may not have liked them initially because you saw in them traits that reminded you of parts of yourself that you have not accepted. This is called psychological projection. Projection is when a person defends themselves against their own unconscious qualities by denying these qualities in themselves while placing them on others. For example, a person who is always angry may accuse other people of being angry and shift the blame onto them in order to avoid facing his or her own anger. It is tricky because sometimes our gut intuition is good, and we know to stay away from someone on the most visceral level. Other times, however, our own issues and defenses get in the way.

As an experiment or exercise, see how many situations trigger a negative emotion every day. You can keep a daily journal of this. The trigger can cause anger, sadness, frustration or pure disgust. Whatever the trigger is, notice it and record it. Breathe and practice acceptance each time this happens and count how many times a day you need to bring awareness to your lack of acceptance. Through practice it will become easier and almost second nature.

Psycho-tips

- Try accepting yourself for better or worse.
- Don't fret if you cannot do this with your family as family dynamics are a huge trigger.
- Try to accept people for who they are without judgment.
- Acceptance does not equal forgiveness.
- If you do not like someone, notice if they are a mirror for a part of you that you have not accepted.
- Bring awareness to the situations in life that you do not accept and be patient with yourself if you have not yet dealt with a traumatic event.
- Journal the situations daily that trigger your negative emotions and become aware of your non-acceptance.

Part Five

Miracles

My Miracle Peacock

*"You get the beauty and
the poop. That's what
God sends us in life. So
you can appreciate the
beauty and clean out
the poop."*
—Zippy Kolsky

Sometimes in our darkest moments we are confronted with an event that makes us "snap out of it." Our mood may have been persistent and enduring, but the event suddenly enables us to shift.

Pay attention to those miraculous moments. Sometimes miracles come in strange ways but help bring us back to the present moment. I recently had this experience.

Although I have worked through the trauma I felt from my 9/11 experience, my sadness and vulnerability were triggered again in June 2016 when I saw an image on television of the plane crashing into the first tower. The flashback made it feel like it just happened yesterday. I immediately prayed for the victims and their families. The image likely affected me more than usual because I had not had enough sleep and I was completely exhausted.

The next day I was still feeling disturbed, but thankfully had some quiet time for prayer, meditation and self-reflection. I had gone out to run a few errands and when I returned home and parked in my driveway, I found a large feather while getting out of the car. We live in the forested area of coastal Connecticut so I was not too surprised by this. It was odd, though, because I had recently picked an Angel Card (referenced in Chapter 12) that said to pay attention to signs and feathers that may come across my path. When I found two more feathers on the driveway, this intrigued me.

When I came into the house, I went right to work at my computer as it served as a great distraction from my sadness. That was when I heard someone banging on the glass door which leads from my kitchen to an outdoor deck. The banging was loud enough that it got my attention and when I went to investigate, I saw that it was not a person but rather an enormous bird pounding the glass with his beak. I was amazed and mesmerized and my cat, Whiskey, and I sat for hours watching him. My other cat, Red, was frightened and hid under the table. The bird's beauty and movement were captivating. What a blessing to see! Then he pooped, not once but four times!

The flashback of 9/11 began to dissipate and hope began to enter into my being. I was excited and sent a video to my husband, Chris, and throughout it kept saying out loud "there's a turkey on our deck!" I said it four times and then when the bird lifted his foot I said over and over in my exaggerated Long Island accent (because I knew it would make Chris laugh), "Look at the paaaaawwwwww, look at the paaaaaawwwww" cracking up as I said it.

It wasn't until I left the house to pick up my clothes at the dry cleaners and showed Eddie, the manager, my video that I heard, "That's not a turkey; that's a peacock!" I was shocked! Then, when I got home and read Chris' email response, he said the same thing. "That's a peacock!" How funny! I really did think it was a turkey because I could not comprehend how a peacock could be banging on my back door. The peacock was still there when I returned from my errands and it stayed the entire day.

I did not want the peacock to leave but he eventually flew away. I had later sent an email out to some friends about it and my friend, Dan, responded that he had seen a random peacock the exact same day on Long Island. What are the chances of this? When I spoke to Animal Control they said the peacock had not escaped from the Arboretum or from anywhere else nearby and no one had reported a lost peacock. It is not clear where this peacock originated. Its appearance felt like a miracle; it lifted my spirits, lifted me out of my sadness and I was now ready to continue with the next steps in my life.

The moral of the story is that even in your most difficult moments, there is only one way it can go when you have hit the bottom and that is up! My hope for you is that you never have those moments, but if you do . . . remember my turkey!

Try to appreciate the beauty of special moments,

even when they come with flaws. Cleaning out the poop is a metaphor for cleaning out your life. This is an important aspect in being able to move forward. It enables us to leave the past behind and create new memories and a peaceful future.

Another experience I am reminded of happened when I met a friend to practice yoga at the beach. The beach was hotter than expected, and since the sun and heat were extreme we decided to do the Warrior Sequence (poses for strength and confidence—as mentioned in Chapter 14) in the water. We began walking on the sandy area in the water, and I suggested that we avoid the little black rocks that were all over. My friend and I noticed that when we stepped on the black rocks they mushed below our feet. We suddenly concluded that they were not rocks at all; they were seagull poop! We froze, screamed and grabbed each other's arms so that we could balance on one leg and avoid stepping on it. It was everywhere and there was no escape. We were literally in the middle of a bunch of mushy excrement. We digressed from yogis to screaming children. It was funny and disgusting all at the same time. There was only one way back to the clean beach and that was by stepping on all of it because every inch was covered. When we got to the beach we were luckily able to wash our feet in the shower, spray them with *peace potion* (sage and other essential oils for cleaning and cleansing—noted in Chapter 12) and continue our yoga. We also had a really good laugh once we were clean!

Perhaps the funniest part of this story is we later

learned that it was not poop at all. When I got home and looked up photos of seagull poop, I realized we were indeed stepping on little black rocks which sunk into the wet, muddy sand. I laughed at the priceless image of two city chicks screaming their way out of what they thought was a disgusting mess.

The theme of the story is that there is good and bad in everything and sometimes things are not what they seem to be. We were at a beautiful beach on a gorgeous day and we got the beauty and the poop. The poop is the past and the beauty is a hopeful and bright future. Let this be a lesson for all of us to continue to clean out and clean up the past so that we can move through it and forward with an abundance of blessings. Also, what we think is the messy part of our lives may actually be an illusion and a blessing in disguise in order to get us to the better part of our lives.

Psycho-tips

- Get plenty of rest so that your resilience levels are at their best.
- Your lowest moments in life are preparing you for your greatest moments in life.
- Allow humor to help dissipate your troubles.
- Clean up the past so you can move forward in your life.
- Believe in yourself and never give up hope.
- You have to move through the mess and not avoid it . . . in order to get to the other side. What may appear to be "poop" may be a blessing in disguise.
- When feeling down remember my turkey and my seagull poop!

A Course In Miracles

by David Asomaning, PhD

"We are all entitled to miracles."
                    —adapted from Lesson 77 of
                    A Course In Miracles

To broaden our topic entitled *Miracles*, I invited my mentor, David Asomaning PhD, to write about *A Course In Miracles*. Dave is the founder of SynchroMind, a leadership development firm. SynchroMind's miracle-minded executive coaching, consulting, and mastermind seminar programs use holistic blends of some of the best entrepreneurial, psychoanalytic, and spiritual disciplines available today. These best practices are used to support miracle-minded leaders, entrepreneurs, CEOs, and people from all walks of life, to design and achieve their highest aspirations synchronistically and miraculously. Dave is also the founder of The Billionaire Life, a division of Synchro-Mind that focuses on leadership development in relation to billionaires.

Dave is a graduate of Yale University where he majored in biology. He has graduate degrees from Hartford Seminary and the Yale Divinity School, together with a diploma in Anglican Studies from Berkeley Divinity

School at Yale, and a teaching certificate from Southern Connecticut State University. He received clinical training in individual, couples, marriage and family, and group psychotherapy and spirituality at The Blanton-Peale Graduate Institute in New York City, where his clinical work focused on synchronicity and the miraculous. In 2003, he completed a PhD in depth psychology and religion at Union Theological Seminary in New York City with a dissertation entitled, *Signs and Wonders: The Relationship Between Synchronicity and the Miraculous in Depth Psychology and Religion.*

The following is an account in his words:

ACIM and My Traumatic Illness

On Monday, February 17, 2014, I was admitted to the emergency room of the main hospital in Vero Beach, Florida, with huge swollen calves, ankles, and feet. For two weeks before this, I had been having difficulty breathing, sleeping, or keeping food down, and I felt a deep abiding inner panic that nothing seemed to quell.

I had no idea what was going on except that I kept thinking my spiritual and psychological work on myself was surfacing some deeply buried trauma. I figured this trauma was related to several claustrophobic panic attacks I had had as a kid, and that I needed to work on some more. Within 24 hours of being in the hospital, I was diagnosed with congestive heart failure and arrhythmia. I was informed I would need open heart surgery to fix a faulty heart valve and correct the arrhythmia.

I was aghast at this diagnosis. I tried to explain to the cardiologists that there had to be some spiritual and psychological explanation for what was happening; and that surely we could approach this whole situation in a more holistic way; that open heart surgery was too radical and was not really called for. I was met by the specialists with firm retorts about the dire consequences, including an increasingly malfunctioning heart and possible death that were awaiting me if I delayed in having the surgery.

As a long time student and teacher of *A Course In Miracles* (ACIM), I knew deep down inside, that what the heart specialists were proposing as the solution to my heart problem, would only really be addressing my symptoms. I knew that the deeper solution involved my applying the principles of ACIM to this impending catastrophe so that I could experience a true miracle of healing and a lasting cure.

Since I was getting nowhere with the cardiologists about my spiritual and psychological approach to my serious heart problems, and they had scheduled my surgery for Friday, February 28, I doubled down to wage a private campaign to turn things around. I realized with dismay that although I was accustomed to using ACIM regularly in my executive coaching work for team building and conflict resolution, I had no confident idea how ACIM might apply to such a catastrophic diagnosis as mine.

I had my laptop with me in the hospital, and so I started researching online what ACIM teaches directly about how to turn such dire medical conditions into miracles. I was convinced that there was a way to experience a miracle in this situation, if only I could find and apply the right principles in the right way before my fast-approaching surgery.

Eventually, in my online research, I came across Judy Edwards Allen's *The Five Stages of Getting Well*, and ordered it through Amazon.com. When it arrived I raced through it, and learned how Allen had applied principles from ACIM to her terminal cancer diagnosis, and had eventually experienced complete remission.

Allen's book helped me zero in on Lesson 136 in ACIM which says "Sickness is a defense against the truth." I was grateful for the guidance her book was providing me on what ACIM taught her about healing from her supposedly terminal illness. However, I was unnerved by the fact that in my almost 20 years of studying and teaching ACIM, I had no real idea about this pivotal lesson. I had no idea how to apply the principles of healing embedded in the lesson so that I could experience a miracle and be healed, and also avoid what I considered to be an unnecessary and, indeed, abhorrent surgery.

In essence, I worked diligently to understand and apply Lesson 136 to my traumatic experience of congestive heart failure, and the impending open heart surgery from which there seemed no escape. I began to understand, dimly at first, then more clearly, that Lesson 136, and Allen's book, were teaching me that I had chosen to be sick in this way on a deep subconscious level. I learned that this sickness was my way of competing with God by proving, through the suffering of my sickness, that I was more powerful than God. I learned that my agenda in all of this was to prove that if I could suffer and even die through this experience, I would have won the power struggle I was in with God.

During one particularly long night in which I wrestled with these emerging understandings, I asked God again, as I had done several times before, why this was happening to me, and what I could do about it. With all my recent study of Allen's book, and her experience with her terminal diagnosis, and my accelerated learning about principles of healing from ACIM, I had become much more open to an answer from God. The answer I heard was that as a teenager I had vowed that I was willing to be crucified as a show of my willingness to follow Jesus no matter the cost. In my conversation with God, I was told that this vow on my part was completely unnecessary, and that I had a deep misunderstanding of what it really means to follow Jesus. I came to understand that my sickness was actually my very distorted way of competing with God and Jesus rather than following them—i.e., that I was using my sickness and suffering to hide and disguise my power struggle with God and Jesus.

The next thing I remember was God telling me that if I would give up my misplaced need to sacrifice myself through crucifixion I would no longer be crucified through the open heart surgery. Upon hearing this, I immediately disavowed all of my earlier years-long dedication to crucifixion, and pledged to follow God and Jesus in truth as I was being helped to understand this.

That night, I went to sleep exhausted with this

intense battle to undo my pledges to suffer, and when I woke up a few hours later in the early morning, I collected my urine as usual in the plastic container I had become quite used to for this purpose. To my horror and deep disappointment, my urine that morning was blood red. Inside, I cried out to God, "How could this be? I've put so much effort into studying ACIM over the last couple of weeks while here in the hospital, in order to experience a miracle, and be healed, and this is the pitiful result of all my work? I now have a new problem with my kidney in addition to my heart problems?" What a nightmare!

I was frustrated, angry, and scared, and was still fuming when the first nurse of the morning came in to check on me. I told her about the blood in my urine, and she passed the news on to the three heart specialists who had been working with me. As each of these specialists came into my room that morning on their rounds, they voiced concern over the blood in my urine, and then admitted that because of this development, it would not be feasible to proceed with the surgery as planned. It then dawned on me that the blood in my urine was a significant miracle in this entire nightmare; that this was God's physical empirical way of getting the medical experts to stand down from their plans for my surgery, where I had failed to convince them with my psycho-spiritual formulations. My mood changed with this realization that my bleeding kidney was God's best way under the circumstances to block the surgery, and that the work I had done in rescinding my vows to suffer crucifixion had been honored almost immediately, although in a way that took me a few hours to understand. WOW!!

I had been scheduled for surgery on Friday, February 28, but now with my right kidney bleeding, the surgery was indeed suspended. This cancellation happened just a couple of days before February 28. What a reprieve!

Due to the fact that the various complications from the congestive heart failure and the arrhythmia (such as way too high heart rate, fluctuating heart rate, vulnerability to blood clots and thus stroke, and also a chance of sudden death from cardiac arrest), had been brought under control by medications, I was sent home on Friday, March 7. The understanding was that the kidney problem would be fixed on an out-patient basis so I could then return for the surgery in several weeks.

I was under doctor's orders to take things very slowly while at home, and to avoid, for example, going up and down any stairs, or doing anything strenuous or stressful, this, given that sometimes, when I had been at my worst, I couldn't even sit upright in a chair in the hospital for more than 5 minutes without beginning to get dizzy on the way to losing consciousness entirely.

The next phase was a busy time seeing various specialists on an out-patient basis to continue working on getting ready for the surgery, while I also continued strengthening my newfound understandings of ACIM and miraculous healing.

In a completely surprising turn of events, I was told on Tuesday, April 4 that due to my improving symptoms, the surgery was probably no longer needed. I was told that this assessment had to be confirmed with an echocardiogram which was done on Wednesday, April 5, and which then confirmed for the three specialists I was seeing that the surgery was no longer called for. This is because my heart rhythm and rate had both gone back to normal, and the damaged valve had also gone back to a mostly normal condition. Also, I no longer had any bleeding from my kidney, and the underlying problem there had become somewhat secondary for the time being.

Also, after about a total of eight weeks off from my regular work schedule, I started to ease back into my executive coaching work.

As you can imagine, I was truly amazed and delighted by this miraculous turn of events, and I am full of joy and gratitude to know that there is definitely a trustworthy way out of the hell of such traumatic torments.

ACIM, Trauma, The Ego, The Body, and Miracles

ACIM teaches that presiding over our stuck-ness in trauma and nightmares is the ego. This is not Freud's ego, or Jung's ego, nor the ego that most people refer to as the harbinger of everyday conceit, narcissism, arrogance, and self-centeredness. ACIM's ego is a brutal, destructive, sinister, malicious, deceptive, and ultimately illusory part of every human mind, and is also the source of each and every collective trauma humanity suffers from: genocide, the threat of nuclear annihilation, war, poverty, racism, social injustice, mass shootings, terrorism, all mental and physical disease, and every other conceivable malaise of any kind. The way out of such nightmarish, yet ultimately, illusory individual and collective trauma of any kind, is through the miraculous healing of the individual and collective negativity contained in the individual and the collective psyche by the Inner Divine Source available to all.

Miracles are the results of shifts in perception through the power of this Divine Source within us, shifts in perception which can solve any problem for us no matter how impossible the problem seems to solve. The physical space-time, energy-matter continuum our bodies are a part of, is an ego-based illusion, which the Divine Source is completely free from. When we tune into the Divine Source, even for a moment, a Holy Instant, we are also free from the limits of the body and the physical world. Understanding and applying all this effectively so that life becomes a consistent series of Holy Instants, takes work and devotion over time, what ACIM refers to as mind training.

In ACIM, psychotherapists at their best are in touch with the Divine Source within, which leads to moments of freedom from all the limits of the ego (Holy Instants). In this way therapists impart this freedom from all limits to their patients and clients, although it is the actual experience of the therapist's freedom from ego limits and trauma that liberates the client rather than the words the therapist speaks. Also, in this way, anyone who is in touch with this state of freedom from ego limits and trauma (even for just a moment), becomes a therapist (whether or not they are actually a psychotherapist), who helps to set others free, in the same way that Allen's experience of freedom from ego and body limits as captured in her book about her miraculous healing helped heal me and to set me free miraculously.

Dave's Psycho-tips

- Develop a daily regimen to use at the start of your day in which you engage in 30 straight days of mental rehearsal using guided meditation, visualization, and/or self-hypnosis audio programs. Let's call this your "30-Day Miracle Campaign."

- Use the following affirmation from Lesson 77 of ACIM in your 30-Day Miracle Campaign: "I am entitled to miracles." This is the underlying approach to my waking up from my traumatic nightmare with congestive heart failure, and this method can be applied to any other trauma, disaster, challenge, problem, or goal in our lives.

- To anchor your 30-Day Miracle Campaign, construct a vision board or treasure map (you can do this digitally with images from Google images on your computer, or on poster board with clippings from magazines), that captures the affirmations and steps being recommended here.

- As part of your 30-Day Miracle Campaign be sure to set clear, ambitious, and measurable goals and represent these on your vision board.

- Incorporate this affirmation into your miracle campaign and onto your vision board: "I am aware of and will undo my negative blueprints (negative repetitive patterns, addictions, toxic beliefs, painful memories, etc.)."
- As part of your 30-Day Miracle Campaign, commit to trusting the guidance, strength, and plan of the Inner Divine Source in everything you think, say, and do, and capture this commitment on your vision board.
- Incorporate affirmations for your optimal health, successful work, financial prosperity, loving relationships, and spiritual enlightenment into your 30-Day Miracle Campaign, and put these affirmations on your vision board.

(Feel free to extend your 30-Day Miracle Campaign to 60 days or 90 days, and to capture your evolving insights onto your vision board as you go along. Creating a digital version of your vision board makes updating it on a regular basis very easy. This also makes it a lot easier to design many different vision boards for different areas of your life, as well as to update them frequently so they stay fresh and relevant.)

28

Office of Miracles

"Allow yourself to be surprised by the miracles all around you."
                    —Barbara Aronica-Buck

Following the chapter by my mentor, Dave Asomaning, I feel compelled to share my own experiences with spiritual signs and miracles. Let me begin by saying that after operating my therapy practice out of a rented office in Greenwich, Connecticut, I later decided to move to my home office which is also my husband's music room. Chris generously allowed me to take over his sanctuary and make it my own. I am thankful for this special space, because it has been home to so many miracles within therapy sessions!

The first time I got a sign that something greater than myself was guiding my therapy sessions was when I heard a chime come out of one of the guitars that hung on the wall. This happened about three years ago, and my client and I both heard it and were amazed. Of course, we agreed that it could not be; we checked all our electronic devices like cell phones, iPad, computer, etc. to see if anything was set to the chime sound. Needless to say, all of our devices were on silent mode, so the chime did not come from one of them. We decided it had to be a sign from angels, but we still had our doubts. After the session finished and my client left, I searched high and low in the music room. I looked at every possible device, guitar tuner, metronome, and anything I could find that could possibly have made the chime sound. I went through the office thoroughly and found nothing. I also asked Chris if he had an alarm or watch that made that sound, and he did not. I still had my doubts.

Miraculous moment number two happened also with a chime, only this time the chime sounded right when the client had an "ah ha" moment. This moment happened to be the most genuine and grounded moment of the entire session. There went the chime. I, of course, had a reaction and told her how special this was and that it had only happened once before. I am not sure if she was a believer, but she went along with the theory that this event was spiritual in nature and came from another dimension. We thought the sound originated from the guitars. Now I know some will argue that the guitars and their strings are always moving and affected by the outside world and a string could easily have made a sound on its own. People seem to try to convince themselves that they are the only ones who exist, though in my heart of hearts I do not believe this. There has to be something greater than us out there whether it is energy, universe, inner self, higher self, spirit guides, God, Jesus, Buddha, Krishna, Mohammad, or Mickey Mouse. It does not matter what your belief is. The belief in a higher being is something that we have been arguing, debating and believing in for centuries.

This brings me to the circumstance of the third chime. Let me set the stage. The third chime happened during a therapy session after I spoke my truth to a client. As therapists we are trained initially in the Freudian view, to listen, not offer any feedback at all, and to just allow the client to free associate (speak freely) in order to bring the unconscious to the conscious. In this method of therapy, we provide interpretations only after having enough information. Many current methods of therapy are geared towards more of a coaching model where the therapist provides feedback throughout the session. In this "quick fix" day and age where people often want answers "now," many clients ask for and appreciate ongoing feedback throughout a session. Providing immediate feedback was valuable to clients in my prior days as a personal fitness trainer, and because I have a compassionate heart, I tend to want to offer feedback, especially if it will provide some relief to the client. Every therapist knows that it is very easy to make the mistake of saying something too soon which can cause the client to have a negative reaction and end treatment prematurely. My husband shared this advice to assess whether it is the right time to speak. "Does it need to be said?", "Does it need to be said now?", and "Does it need to be said now by me?" I have used this guidance since the day he first mentioned it and have also shared it with clients; it is extremely valuable in judging when to keep one's mouth shut. In Kripalu Yoga there is a similar questioning: "Is it kind?", "Is it necessary?", "Is it truthful?" These are wise things to think about before speaking.

Amazingly, the third chime occurred at the exact moment that I shared my thoughts with my client, voicing my concerns about his situation and telling him he deserved better. Boom, chime! I spoke from the heart, but given the delicate nature of knowing when to speak or when to just listen I hesitated, because I only wanted the best approach for him. We both agreed that sharing my thoughts at that time was helpful. The chime, in a spiritual setting, seemed like an affirmation.

Recently I was working with a client who carried an enormous amount of grief and fear. She wondered if her deceased loved ones were always with her. We had talked about this in previous sessions and concluded that it is comforting to believe in their presence especially if it helps us cope on a daily basis. This time I also said that "we have no proof and we will unfortunately never really know for sure."

Well, because I questioned the existence of those spirits, what followed next felt like I had caused an enormous upset in their world. For the next twenty five minutes as we proceeded with a talk therapy session the lights flickered continually. It was difficult to ignore and we initially blamed it on a possible approaching storm or a problem with the central air conditioning. As soon as we started to make excuses, my digital printer (which had been turned off) suddenly went on, and the light flashed on the display. I felt like I was in the movie *Ghost* when

Patrick Swayze as a ghost sends messages to the computers of his former friend (and eventual accomplice to his murder) to scare him. I do not believe the spirits were trying to scare us. However, I do believe they were trying to get our attention and leave us with the message that they are always with us if we just pay attention.

After the printer went on and off, my client and I were anxious. She said a prayer for protection even though I assured her that my office was sacred and safe. Once we both relaxed, all the flickering of the lights suddenly stopped. It became still and serene, and we spoke about the amazing experience we had just shared.

At the end of the session, I walked my client to her car and we both noticed that the outside world seemed more peaceful, the flowers were filled with brilliant bright colors, the trees and forest were greener and for a moment we both felt like we were in a dream, not really here. Oddly enough, at the same time we both felt very much here, more present and aware than ever before. The best way for me to explain is that we felt like it was just the two of us, and the world around us was painted in the most beautiful way, almost like a fairytale.

Psycho-tips

- Trust in the universe or God, whatever your beliefs are . . . TRUST.
- Have faith that things will work out in a matter of time.
- Be open to miracles and pay attention.
- Turn fearfulness into peacefulness by remaining calm.
- Notice the signs around you from the universe.
- Take in the colors of the flowers, forest and all of nature around you. Allow it to permeate your being.
- Step away from judgment of what is occurring and just allow it to occur.

Part Six

Spirituality and Religion

Mind Body Soul Service:
Temple Beth El, Stamford, Connecticut

"Kol Ha-neshamah T'hallel Yah" -
"Every Breath Celebrates the Source of Life."
        —Leonard Felder, PhD (Author of
        More Fully Alive: The Benefits of
        Using Jewish Wisdom for Responding
        to Stress and Overload.)

In October of 2012, Cantor George Mordecai, the former Cantor of Temple Beth El in Stamford, Connecticut, approached me about doing a collaboration of a yoga class and a Kirtan, which is a Sanskrit word that refers to a narrating of beliefs through songs or chants. This was the beginning of a spiritual endeavor at Temple Beth El where I introduced yoga to people who had never experienced it before. It was also part of a newly created program that combined prayer with yoga.

Combining yoga with a religious orientation was experiential and we were able to see what worked and what did not. Overall it was favorably accepted and many in the community benefited from the new format I helped to create. Blessings are sent to Cantor Mordecai who moved on to a new synagogue where he continues his lifelong passion and dedication to his Jewish faith and spirituality.

After Cantor Mordecai left Temple Beth El, I continued the tradition of the yoga class. Periodically there are times when I am not available to teach the class because my psychotherapy practice takes precedence. I found two wonderful substitute teachers, Monica Keady and Ilene Friedman, to fill in for me when I cannot be there. They have a Zen-like calming nature, which is a nice offset to my energetic dancelike orientation.

As a result of our yoga class, our new Cantor, Cantor Magda Fishman, from Chapter 23, approached me about doing a *Mind Body Soul Service* for a Friday evening Shabbat (day of rest) service. In collaboration with Rabbi Joshua Hammerman, Katie Kaplan (soprano diva), and Cantor Fishman (mezzo-soprano diva and fabulous trumpet and percussion player), we created the first service of its kind at Temple Beth El. It was divine, lovely and special for all who were involved. When the three of us first sang *Elohai N'tzor* (based on Psalm 34:14) at the conclusion of the *Amidah* (silent prayer), it was a beautiful and special moment that I will always treasure. Rabbi Hammerman's spiritual expertise and Katie Kaplan's knowledge of *The Jewish Renewal Movement* added an extra element of passion and prayer to the service. I offered yoga and meditation which was appropriate for all ages and could be done even by people who wanted to stay seated in a chair.

Through this experience, I noticed that the Jewish religion and the practice of yoga correlate nicely. The stance taken during certain Hebrew prayers, particularly during the Amidah is similar to Tadasana (Mountain Pose) practiced in yoga. Also during the Amidah prayer, there are times when the congregation bows in respect to God. Similarly in yoga we bow into a forward fold called Uttanasana. The bow is out of respect and gratitude for our many blessings. In yoga we strive for full embodiment or oneness of body, mind and spirit. Similarly, in the Jewish religion when we sway while *davening* (the Yiddish word for prayer) this allows us to take the prayers into our body and into our entire being. King David writes in Psalm 35:10, "All of my limbs shall proclaim: Who is like You . . ." when we pray in Judaism, we pray with all of our being.

The experience of combining prayer with yoga has been enlightening, and I am grateful that Rabbi Hammerman asked me to continue the tradition of teaching yoga to the congregation for more Friday evening services. It is my gift and privilege to offer this to the congregation.

In the previous chapters, there is the mention of "signs" from the universe or God. One day, the yoga class I offer at the temple was moved into the sanctuary as the room we usually used for class was occupied. In the quiet sanctuary during a yoga sequence called a sun salutation when we raised our arms upward to the heavens, I noticed one of the seven branch menorahs by the arc where the Torahs (Holy Scriptures) were kept flashed at me. No one else in the class noticed it but one yogi said that the light was winking at me. These are the precious miraculous moments of life. If you pay attention, you may see things that no one else sees.

Psycho-tips

- No matter what spiritual practice you observe, when you pray . . . pray with your entire being.
- The body-mind connection can be adapted to any spiritual practice.
- You can do yoga from a chair (or a standing position) and still receive all the benefits from the practice.
- Religion does not have to segregate people. An egalitarian synagogue such as Temple Beth El in Stamford, Connecticut welcomes everyone and is open to experiential practices of yoga, renewal and Kirtan (songs or chants).
- Yoga and Hinduism have a belief in monotheism; the belief is in one God with many faces, not in multiple Gods.
- Practice being open minded when it comes to religion and spirituality.
- If none of this resonates with you, disregard it with a non-judgmental stance of respect and appreciation.

30

Prayer

"My prayers at the Holy Wall in Jerusalem have
always been answered. I never asked for much,
but what I prayed for did happen . . . God listens."
−Irwin B. Gerber

Prayer can be one of the most powerful mental health interventions. Many psychologists, psychiatrists, psychotherapists, life coaches and teachers stay away from "prayer" because they associate it with religion. However, prayer just means intention. As stated in Chapter 23, it can be a prayer to the universe, a prayer to your higher self, to your spirit guides, to nature, or whatever you believe in. The power of prayer is that it sets energy in motion and creates action. It can begin with gratitude for what is working in your life and can even stop there. Gratitude is an expression of appreciation for all that is. If we look at our lives through the lens of gratitude, we can begin to appreciate what we do have instead of focusing on what we want.

There is a difference between what we want and what we need. Pray for what you need by thanking God in advance for blessings of abundance and be grateful for what you already have. In this way you are seeing yourself as abundant instead of lacking. Setting an intention such as, "My intention is to inspire people with the genuine words I have written" can allow things to flow in that direction. I encourage my clients to keep a gratitude journal with one or many things written each day that they are grateful for. For me, gratitude, intention and prayer all go together. In my own experience, praying out loud has been the most powerful form of prayer. Also, singing out loud seems to connect with higher vibrations of energy because of the magnitude of the sound. Think of the opera singer breaking the glass from singing the highest note. The vibration raises with your voice and higher vibrations can bring about greater miracles. I am not providing any scientific evidence on this front and wish to state that this is all theory and what has worked for me personally and sometimes in my practice. I pray out loud with clients, state positive intentions, and welcome anyone including atheist, agnostic, and all religious beliefs. No matter what your belief, the intention is to set movement in motion and to be able to receive an abundance of blessings.

In the Reiki 1 Teaching Manual I had created for students I offer some of my favorite prayers. Reiki, according to the *International Center for Reiki Training,* is a Japanese technique for stress reduction and relaxation that also promotes healing. I became a Reiki Master in 2010 and primarily use it at the end of my yoga classes during the ending meditation which is called Savasana or Corpse Pose. The form of Reiki I am trained in is Usui Shiki Ryoho which comes through a spiritual lineage of Mikao Usui,

Chujiro Hayashi, Hawayo Takata and Phyllis Lei Furumoto. The term Reiki broken down means, Rei "Higher Power" and Ki "Energy." It is a gentle, meditative light touch coming from love that allows the person receiving to awaken and ignite their own healing. Some of the Reiki music and prayers have helped me on my journey up to this point. As I move forward, my further study is now guided on the path of Judaism and Zen Buddhism. I am Jewish by birth and I love the melodies, traditions and prayers from my Jewish heritage. I follow the spiritual aspects of my religion more than laws.

Here are some of the prayers I incorporated in my Reiki Level 1 Teaching Manual:

The Reiki Principals

Just for today I release all worry.
Just for today I release all anger.
Just for today I shall earn my living with integrity.
Just for today I will be kind to every living thing.
Just for today I will give thanks
for all my many blessings.

The Serenity Prayer

God grant me the serenity
To accept the things I cannot change;
Courage to change the things I can;
And wisdom to know the difference.

Living one day at a time;
Enjoying one moment at a time;
Accepting hardships as the pathway to peace;
Taking, as He did, the sinful world
As it is, not as I would have it;
Trusting that He will make all things right
If I surrender to His will;
So that I may be reasonably happy in this life
And supremely happy with Him
Forever and ever in the next.
—Reinhold Niebuhr

Psalm 23
A Psalm of David

The LORD is my shepherd; I shall not be in want.
He makes me lie down in green pastures;
he leads me beside quiet waters,
He restores my soul. He guides me in paths
of righteousness for his name's sake.
Even though I walk through the valley of the shadow
of death, I will fear no evil, for you are with me;
your rod and your staff, they comfort me.
You prepare a table before me in the presence
of my enemies. You anoint my head with oil;
my cup overflows.
Surely goodness and love will follow me in
all the days of my life, and I will dwell in the
house of the LORD forever.
Amen

Archangel Michael's Illusion Prayer

"I will not allow this illusion to separate me from
my peace. Archangel Michael intervene, and
dissolve this situation into divine right order.
Under God's law of grace IT IS DONE."
–Katie Russell

Reiki Prayer

"Guide me and heal me so that I can be
of greater service to others."
–Theresa Joseph

Protection Prayer

"We only invite love, light and God.
Any darkness that tries to enter
we refuse and rebuke."
–Pamela

Gratitude Prayer
"Dear God,
Thank you for all the blessings you have given us that we
sometimes take for granted. Thank you for the eyes we
see with, the ears we hear with, the nose we smell with,
the tongue we taste with and the hands we touch with.
Thank you for our ability to help those in need. Thank
you for our heart which is filled with loving compassion."
–Pamela

Other prayers you may use are the *Shema Yisrael* from Judaism or *The Lord's Prayer* from Christianity.

It is basically up to you to decide which prayers resonate with you. You may also make up your own prayer or best way of connecting to the universe, God or to your inner-self. You would be surprised how prayers can come to you when your mind is still enough to listen and allow. I have one client who calls herself the *Prayer Warrior* and I agree with this title as she prays from the heart so easily and effortlessly. One of her prayers sounds something like this:

Prayer Warrior

"Lord,
I ask you to come with me and help me get centered,
I ask you to be with my family and those in need,
I ask that those in need find comfort,
I ask that you be with me and help me with
my ailments which make me agitated and annoyed.
I am having a hard time.
Please give me the strength Lord,
Other people are having problems also,
Help me to reach out of myself as a *Prayer Warrior*
so that I can be with them.
I thank you for my special friends.
Thank you for helping me soothe and
calm the ripples in the water.
With your hand on my shoulder allow people

to contact me to give them strength,
I need you and ask you to be there for me.
Thank you for Pam and our time together,
For her responding to my emails
even when it's not our time.
Thank you for loving me when
I'm not feeling very lovable.
I love you!"
–Prayer Warrior

"May you be blessed with an abundance
of health, wealth, love, light and joy!"
–Pamela

Psycho-tips

- Include gratitude within your prayers.
- Keep a gratitude journal.
- Pray as if you have already received an abundance of blessings.
- Pray out loud.
- Sing your prayers.
- Be still enough to connect to what your spirit is asking.
- Allow prayers to come to you and through you by being open and receptive. Be still enough to receive the prayer.

31

Smile As a Cover Up

"The loneliest people are the kindest. The saddest people smile the brightest. The most damaged people are the wisest . . . all because they do not wish to see anyone else suffer the way they do."
–Anonymous

The above quote about the saddest people smiling the brightest brings us to the issue of *Spiritual Bypassing*. Spiritual bypassing is when you cover up your deepest issues with spirituality, religion, career or social mask. There are two songs that portray this concept beautifully. One is *Smile* composed by Charlie Chaplan with lyrics by John Turner and Geoffrey Parsons and the other is *Put on a Happy Face* from the musical *Bye Bye Birdie*, composed by Charles Strouse with lyrics written by Lee Adams.

In both songs the lyrics recommend covering up your sadness with a big smile. This may remind you of a time in your youth when you were crying and a teacher or parent told you to stop. The learned behavior of smiling to cover up pain, sadness or trauma is a good skill to have in social situations, although it can become problematic if you never deal with the issues that lie beneath the smile. Physiologically when you smile, you can change your overall mood in the moment; however the underlying issues still remain.

I have a supervisor from my Somatic Experiencing® training who I enjoy working with named Roger Saint-Laurent. The first few times we worked together he knew right away that the bigger my smile was, the tougher the session would be. It is funny because people tell me all the time that they love my smile and that I should always "keep smiling." However, I learned that a smile can be a cover for the hurt that is underneath. In order to not bypass our deepest wounds, we all need to address, face and work through the issues that are below the surface. The work is ongoing, but gets easier over time and helps us to grow as individuals.

There are many forms of spiritual bypassing which can be used as great short term coping mechanisms. Prayer and spirituality can help you rise above situations, but may also bypass some of the deeper psychological issues. When using spirituality and prayer, understand and be aware that if you have not gone deeper to address what is going on inside, it can backfire. Many conflicts occur in spiritual institutions because of this very reason. Therefore, if you use prayer, meditation, Reiki, yoga, religion, or anything else as a way to find peace, it is advised to complement it with some psychological work.

Being in a spiritual leadership role has many challenges when considering the topic of spiritual bypassing. The ego can sometimes get in the way and make you feel that you are above others because of your powerful role and training. However, having this position does not mean that you are dismissed from doing the work that is needed deep within the psyche. In Robert August Masters book entitled *Spiritual Bypassing*, he thoroughly describes and addresses these issues without disrespect to anyone in these leadership or clergy positions. Many people use spiritual bypassing to cover up their issues. It can work for a while until there is an interpersonal conflict, grief, a relationship issue or a crisis and everything falls apart, and your so called "true colors" come out. If you have not done the psychological work to address your deepest wounds and traumas, your spirituality will not save you in times of grief or crisis.

I actually had an incident like this in my early twenties with one of my former spiritual teachers from California. I studied under this teacher and in a spiritual setting we had a mutually loving and connected relationship. One day, though, we had a personal conflict and a difference of opinion. We engaged in a heated exchange, and I realized later that we both had underlying wounds that needed deeper psychological work that the spiritual guidance could not provide. It was after this incident that I became acutely aware of what spiritual bypassing meant and began studying it on a more intimate level. I wanted to more fully understand what had happened in the conflict we had. I realized that I had put my teacher on a pedestal, expected only the best from her and had idealized her spiritual talent and experience. Unfortunately, this idealization is all too common within the relationship between teachers and students. Since this experience,

I prefer to call my yoga students "fellow yogis" and I prefer for them to call me "Yogi Pam" instead of "teacher." Additionally, I like to refer to my superiors as mentors rather than teachers. It helps to remove the expectation that the teacher will be perfect and suggests they are on the same level as the student, in an equal relationship. I do my best to not refer to myself as a teacher, but more as a guide, mentor, therapist, supervisor and guardian angel.

One psychological and spiritual tool that you can use on your own to go deeper and avoid bypassing is to practice meditation. I am learning to do my meditation in silence and recently became a member of the *New York Zen Center for Contemplative Care* where silent meditation is offered. In my previous meditations I would listen to Reiki music. It is lovely, angelic music that enabled me to rise above most situations and connect to "the clouds." However, I realized that in silent Zen meditation, I go much deeper into my psyche and become much more intimate with ME. Over time and with practice every day, I am learning that the silence can actually be delicious!

Challenge yourself to become familiar with your body and self and to not bypass those uncomfortable areas. What feels dissonant right now may be your path to a more connected relationship with all parts of yourself.

Psycho-tips

- When you just "smile," notice if you are using it to cover up your issues.
- Be aware if you are using your spirituality to cope with deep psychological issues, and if this is the case, bring your attention to it.
- Work with a professional on your psychological traumas.
- Bring awareness to your ego and notice if you are putting yourself above people instead of being one with them.
- Refer to your teachers as mentors and supervisors, which will lessen some of the idealization and the need for them to be perfect.
- If you are using a powerful career to feel good about yourself, you may be avoiding turning inward to work on your psychological issues and psyche. Try to become more connected with who you really are outside of your mask and title.
- Try meditating in silence.

Part Seven

Closing
Sentiments

32

Till We Meet Again

"Taking care of myself is a big job. No wonder I avoided it for so long."
                                    —Anonymous

I leave you with this last story. As I was getting my Master's degree, I worked diligently in my studio apartment in Battery Park City for hours at a time writing papers and completing coursework. I had a desk chair that I had acquired from a thrift shop and always felt that the energy in that chair gave me the inspiration and motivation to write from the heart. I could literally sit for twelve hours straight on that chair and the words just flowed on the paper. I always attributed my academic success to the chair. I thought that the person who had previously owned the chair must have been a brilliant scholar! I cannot believe I gave that chair away when I later moved to a smaller apartment on the East Side of Manhattan. The apartment barely fit me, Snowflake, and all my boxes, so I could not keep the chair too. I gave it away, never to think about it again until now.

In writing this book, I realized that it was not the chair that inspired me and gave me my perseverance. It was me all along! Much like with meditation, if we just sit still and allow Divine wisdom to flow through us, our own beautiful individual light will shine.

At the beginning of this book, I spoke about owning my power. I had a tough time doing that for a brutally long period. This time when I sat to write this book, I was ready to take it on and the ideas flowed freely. I now realize that the power to finish this project was within me all along. I had the wisdom and knowledge to do it. I just needed the confidence, trust and faith to carry out the task. My belief is that this book was guided to me through my divinity, and Dave Asomaning's chapter on miracles confirms how this is possible.

Speaking of Divine intervention, my printer just turned on from the off position and the digital display flashed at the exact moment that I wrote that last sentence! WOW!!!

Thank you for being on this journey with me. Thank you for allowing me to write from my heart and to be received with open arms without judgment. Thank you for having the courage to take the first step toward looking within yourself instead of looking outside for your truth. Thank you for being responsible, reliable, trustworthy, compassionate and kind. Thank you for your sincerity, intelligence, passion and love. It is my deepest and most humble gift to be able to share this work with you. There is joy mixed with sadness, fear mixed with hope, trauma mixed with laughter, and uncertainty mixed with love. It is my hope that you can move and flow between these opposite states with a sense of purpose and freedom.

May you live a life filled with genuine connections and be in service with love and nurturance for humanity. May you find the space between the lines and ride the beautiful waves with ease and grace as you continue your path to *Healing Trauma from the Inside Out*.

Blessings, Love and Light . . . till we meet again,

Namaste . . .

Pamela

About The Author

 Pamela Tinkham, MSW, LCSW, RYT®, C-IAYT, is a Licensed Clinical Social Worker, a somatic therapist and a Yoga-Psychotherapist. She holds a Master's degree in Social Work from Fordham University where she graduated with honors, and a Bachelor of Arts degree in Dance from Butler University. She also holds national certifications from The Yoga Alliance, the American College of Sports Medicine, and the American Council on Exercise. She was certified as a Reiki Master in 2010.

Pamela has been working with clients on their health goals since 1992 and added the clinical therapy piece to her practice in 2004. She is licensed in Connecticut, New York, and Idaho. Her Connecticut clinical license and years of experience enable her to educate and supervise students and entry level therapists as well.

In 2007, Pamela created Mind Body Fitness, LLC, the combination of fitness and mental health, after working as the Director of Behavioral Health at a medical practice in Westchester, NY. Pamela exited the fitness world in 2012 to solely focus on yoga-psychotherapy. She amended her LLC to Pamela Tinkham, LLC and continues to treat individuals, couples, and teens with various mental health issues including trauma.

Pamela's achievements include the completion of SEP (Somatic Experiencing Practitioner) in 2017 at the Somatic Experiencing® Trauma Institute SE™. She was acknowledged in Book Two of *The Intelligent Divorce* by Mark R. Banschick, MD. She wrote a guest blog in *Psychology Today* entitled, *Stress Busters . . . Yoga and Exercise.* She was published in *Stamford Plus Magazine* for the article, *Soulmates, The Psychological Relationship Between Us and Our Pets and How They Keep Us Sane.* She was also published in *Making Marriage a Success* by Jaleh Donaldson. She had a televised Interview on *Good Day New York* about women's bodies and women's health. She presented *"Conquering Depression: Not a Way Out . . . a Way Through"* lecture and *"Conquering Teen Depression: Navigating Around the Pressures of Social Media"* and she had the honor of being the fitness trainer for Queen Noor upon her visit to NYC from Jordan.

Pamela runs her practice out of Stamford, Connecticut.

www.PamelaTinkham.com
pamelatinkham@gmail.com

About The Editor

 Linda Mortenson offers her wisdom and expertise as a writer and editor in her ongoing philanthropic endeavors. She is currently Chief Financial Officer and Vice President for the charitable organization, Hope for Education Ghana Inc., which funds educational scholarships for high school and college students in Ghana. Linda has written and edited the narrations on the organization's website and also its proposals for grants.

Linda holds an MBA in Finance from New York University where she graduated with honors. She also holds a BS degree in Accounting from SUNY Binghamton where she graduated summa cum laude.

Linda wrote and edited research reports on a regular basis as a Managing Director at Oppenheimer Capital where she worked for fifteen years as an Equity Research Analyst and Portfolio Manager. The reports covered industry analysis and individual company reviews. She also wrote reports on various accounting topics.

Linda also volunteered at her son's school and with the following charities: Visiting Neighbors, God's Love We Deliver and The Friends Shelter. She embraced the opportunity to assist in editing Pamela's book and supports Pamela's mission of wanting to inspire people to heal from their traumas and find inner peace.

References

Introduction

Ajaya, S. (1983). *Psychotherapy East and West: a Unifying Paradigm.* Honesdale, PA: The Himalayan International Institute.

Perez, K. (2001). *Social Work in the Era of Devolution.* New York, NY: Fordham University Press.

Chapter 1

DateWorks (2016). *Zen, a 16-Month 2017 Calendar,* Indianapolis, IN: Trends International, LLC.

Levine, P. (1997). *Waking the Tiger: Healing Trauma.* Berkeley, CA: North Atlantic Books.

Marlock, G, Weiss, H, Young, C, Soth, M. (2015). *The Handbook of Body Psychotherapy & Somatic Psychology.* Berkeley, CA: North Atlantic Books.

USABP, (2016). *United States Association for Body Psychotherapy, The Hub of Somatic Psychology,* http://usabp.org/.

Chapter 2

Beck, A. (1976). *Cognitive Therapy And The Emotional Disorders.* New York, NY: Penguin Books.

Crossley, J. (2013). *Personal Training Theory and Practice.* New York, NY: Routledge.

Ellis, A. (2001). *New Directions for Rational Emotive Behavioral Therapy: Overcoming Destructive Beliefs, Feelings, and Behaviors.* New York, NY: Prometheus Books.

Marlock, G, Weiss, H, Young, C, Soth, M. (2015). *The Handbook of Body Psychotherapy & Somatic Psychology.* Berkeley, CA: North Atlantic Books.

Saleebey, D. (2002). *The Strengths Perspective in Social Work Practice, 3rd Edition.* Boston, MA: Pierson Education Company.

Yalom, I. (1980). *Existential Psychotherapy.* New York, NY: Basic Books.

Yalom, I. (2002*). The Gift of Therapy*. New York, NY: HarperCollins Publishers.

Chapter 3

https://www.goodreads.com/author/quotes/56230.Howard_Thurman

Kabat-Zinn, J, Segal, Z, Teasdale, J, Williams, M. (2007). *The Mindful Way through Depression: Freeing Yourself from Chronic Unhappiness.* New York, NY: The Guilford Press.

Kabat-Zinn, J. (1994). *Wherever You Go There You Are: Mindfulness Meditation in Everyday Life.* New York, NY: Hachette Books.

Thurman, H. (1976). *Jesus and the Disinherited.* Boston, Massachusetts: Beacon Press Books.

Chapter 4

American Psychiatric Association (2013). *Diagnostic and Statistical Manual of Mental Disorders, Fifth Edition, DSM 5- TM.* Washington, DC: American Psychiatric Association.

Chapter 5

May, R. (1977). *The Meaning of Anxiety.* New York, NY: W. W. Norton & Company, Inc.
http://www.tilakpyle.com/sanskrit.htm

Chapter 7

Corsini, R. (2002). *The Dictionary of Psychology.* New York, NY: Brunner- Routledge.
Crossley, J. (2013). *Personal Training Theory and Practice.* New York, NY: Routledge. Levine, P. (2008). *Healing Trauma.* (p. 40). Boulder, CO: Sounds True, Inc.
Levine, P. (1997). *Waking the Tiger: Healing Trauma.* (p. 63). Berkeley, CA: North Atlantic Books.
Marlock, G, Weiss, H, Young, C, Soth, M. (2015). *The Handbook of Body Psychotherapy & Somatic Psychology.* Berkeley, CA: North Atlantic Books.
https://www.goodreads.com/author/quotes/8750.Jon_ Kabat_Zinn
USABP, (2016). *United States Association for Body Psychotherapy, The Hub of Somatic Psychology,* http://usabp.org/.

Chapter 8

Hamblin, J. (2016). *The Atlantic. Why One Neuroscientist Started Blasting His Core,* August 24, 2016 issue.
http://www.pnas.org/ (journal of the National Academy of Sciences)
http://www.iayt.org/?page=ContemporaryDefinition yogatherapy

Hubbs, A. (2012). *Empower Yoga Teacher Training Manual*, Mantra Mind Body. New York, NY.

Levine, P. (2010). *In An Unspoken Voice: How the Body Releases Trauma and Restores Goodness.* (p.88). Berkeley, CA: North Atlantic Books.

Satchidananda, S. (1988). *The Living Gita: the Complete Bhagavad Gita.* Buckingham, VA: Satchidananda Ashram —Yogaville, Inc.

Chapter 9

Dyer, W. (2009). *Excuses Begone! How to Change Lifelong, Self-Defeating Thinking Habits.* New York, NY: Hay House Inc.

http://www.zen-buddhism.net/practice/zen-meditation.html

Levine, P. (1997). *Waking the Tiger: Healing Trauma.* Berkeley, CA: North Atlantic Books.

www.Reiki.org

Satchidananda, S. (2011). *The Yoga Sutras of Patanjali.* Buckingham, VA: Satchidananda Ashram, Integral Yoga Publications.

Chapter 10

Faulds, D. (2006). *From Root to Bloom, Yoga Poems and Other Writings.* Kearney, NE: Morris Publishing.

Forbes, B. (2011). *Yoga For Emotional Balance: Simple Practices to Help Relieve Anxiety and Depression.* (p.72). Boston, MA: Shambhala Publications, Inc.

Hubbs, A. (2012). *Empower Yoga Teacher Training Manual*, Mantra Mind Body. New York, NY.

http://www.yogajournal.com/article/global/pranayama/

Chapter 11

Hubbs, A. (2012). *Empower Yoga Teacher Training Manual*, Mantra Mind Body. New York, NY.

https://www.goodreads.com/author/quotes/5867530.Sri_Aurobindo

http://www.yogajournal.com/article/beginners/the-eight-limbs/

Satchidananda, S. (2011). *The Yoga Sutras of Patanjali.* Buckingham, VA: Satchidananda Ashram, Integral Yoga Publications.

Chapter 12

Alcoholics Anonymous (1952). *Twelve Steps and Twelve Traditions.* New York, NY: Alcoholics Anonymous World Services, Inc.

Beck, J. (1995). *Cognitive Therapy: Basics and Beyond.* New York, NY: The Guilford Press.

Farmer, S. Card Deck: *Messages from your Animal Spirit Guides*.

http://jungcurrents.com/quotations

http://spiritualityhealth.com/articles/ancient-art-smudging

http://www.livestrong.com/article/248511-benefits-of-a-hot-vinegar-bath/

Levin, D. Card Deck. *Zen Cards*.

Levine, P. (2010). *In An Unspoken Voice: How the Body Releases Trauma and Restores Goodness.* (p.88). Berkeley, CA: North Atlantic Books.

Levine, P. (2008). *Healing Trauma.* (p.114). Boulder, CO: Sounds True, Inc.

Pearce, M. Card Deck: *Horse Spirit Cards*.

Peschek-Bohmer, F, Schreiber, G. (2002). *Healing Crystals and Gemstones: From Amethyst to Zircon, A comprehensive listing of the therapeutic uses and healing effects of the most important crystals and gemstones.* Old Saybrook, CT: Konecky & Konecky.

Seligman, M. (2002). *Authentic Happiness: Using the New Positive Psychology to Realize Your Potential for Lasting Fulfillment.* New York, NY: Free Press.

Tinkham, P., (2016). *Healing Trauma From the Inside Out.* Chp.27, *A Course In Miracles by David Asomaning PhD.* https://www.createspace.com/.

Virtue, D. Card Decks: *Messages from your Angels, Magical Messages from your Fairies, Goddess Guidance Cards, Ascended Masters Cards, Daily Guidance from your Angels, Archangel Michael Cards.*

www.whitesagewellness.com

Chapter 13

American Psychiatric Association (2013). *Diagnostic and Statistical Manual of Mental Disorders, Fifth Edition, DSM 5-TM.* Washington, DC: American Psychiatric Association.

Bentley, K, Walsh, J. (2013). *The Social Worker and Psychotropic Medication.* Belmont, CA: Brooks/Cole.

http://ajp.psychiatryonline.org/doi/pdf/10.1176/appi.ajp. 2015.1720501

Chapter 14

Campbell, J, Osbon, D. (1991). *Reflections on the Art of Living, A Joseph Campbell Companion.* New York, NY: HarperCollins Publishers.

Geweniger-Bohlander (2014). *Pilates, A Teacher's Manual.* Heidelberg, Berlin: Springer Publishing.

Hubbs, A. (2012). *Empower Yoga Teacher Training Manual,* Mantra Mind Body. New York, NY.

https://thebuddhistcentre.com/text/loving-kindness-meditation

http://www.collective-evolution.com/2014/03/15/scientists-quanitfy-graphically-chart-energy-of-human-chakras-in-various-emotional-states/, Waliamarch, A.

Long, R. (2008). *The Key Poses of Yoga.* China: Banda Yoga Publications, LLC.

Pond, D. (1999). *Chakras For Beginners: A guide to Balancing Your Chakra Energies.* Woodbury, MN: Llewellyn Publications.

Virtue, D. (1998). *Chakra Clearing: Awakening Your Spiritual Power to Know and Heal.* Carlsbad, CA: Hay House Inc.

www.ouramazingworld.org/spirituality/the-7-chakras-the-basics-explored-for-beginners

www.yogafordepression.com

Chapter 15

Beck, A. (1976). *Cognitive Therapy And The Emotional Disorders.* New York, NY: Penguin Books.

Faulds, R. (2006). *Kripalu Yoga: A Guide to Practice On and Off the Mat.* New York: Bantam.

Gibbs, N. (2016). TIME: *Mindfulness: The New Science of Health and Happiness*. New York, NY: Time Inc. Books.

Goleman, D. (1988). *The Meditative Mind: The Varieties of Meditative Experience*. New York, NY: Penguin Putnam, Inc.

Hanson, R. (2009). *Buddha's Brain: The Practical Neuroscience of Happiness, Love & Wisdom*. Oakland, CA: New Harbinger Publications Inc.

Hirschi, G. (2000). *Mudras: Yoga in your Hands*. San Francisco, CA: Red Wheel/Weisler, LLC.

https://kripalu.org/resources/brfwa-prescription

http://www.mindful.org/jon-kabat-zinn-defining-mindfulness/

Kabat-Zinn, J, Segal, Z, Teasdale, J, Williams, M. (2007). *The Mindful Way through Depression: Freeing Yourself from Chronic Unhappiness*. New York, NY: The Guilford Press.

Linehan, M. (1993). *Skills Training Manual for Treating Borderline Personality Disorder*. New York, NY: Guilfore Publications, Inc.

http://www.soundstrue.com/ (Mindfulness Based Stress Reduction).

Chapter 16

Levine, P. (1997). *Waking the Tiger: Healing Trauma*. Berkeley, CA: North Atlantic Books.

Tinkham, P. (2008). Stamford Plus Magazine, *Soulmates, The psychological relationship between us and our pets and how they can keep us sane*, Fall, 2008, Stamfordplus.com.

www.psychologytoday.com

Chapter 17

Lykken, D. PhD. https://en.wikipedia.org/wiki/David

Oaklander, M. (2016). *The New Science of Exercise*. TIME, September.

Grant, A. (2013). Give and Take: *Why Helping Others Drives Our Success*. Penguin Books.

www.helpguide.org/articles/exercise-fitness/emotional -benefits-of-exercise.htm, *Emotional Benefits of Exercise*.

www.ncbi.nlm.nih.gov/pmc/articles/PMC1470658, *Exercise for Mental Health*.

www.mayoclinic.org/diseases:conditions/depression/in-depth/depression-and-exercise/art-20046495. *Depression and Anxiety: Exercise Eases Symptoms*.

Weir, K. (2011). *The Exercise Effect*. American Psychological Association. Cover story, Dec.2011, Vol 42, No. 11.

http://rightcarealliance.org/cms/assets/uploads/2015/10/ Mission-Statement-on-RCA-Website.pdf

Metzl, J. (2014). *Exercise as Medicine: Trends in Preventive Wellness Through Activity*.

Chapter 18

Beck, A. (1976). *Cognitive Therapy And The Emotional Disorders.* New York, NY: Penguin Books.

http://www.yogajournal.com/article/beginners/the-eight-limbs/

http://www.globalhealingcenter.com/natural-health/ how-unhealthy-is-white-flour/

https://www.ekhartyoga.com/blog/the-niyamas-bringing-saucha-into-your-life

https://www.google.com/search?q=iyengar+quote+on+sauc
ha&biw=1680&bih=920&tbm=isch&tbo=u&source=univ
&sa=X&ved=0ahUKEwiE1o3OrbDQAhVH-
mMKHXSHCa0QsAQIHQ#imgrc=EgQZkAqZ_Z39kM%3A

Chapter 19

https://itunes.apple.com/us/album/les-miserables-original-
broadway/id1081609832
Long, R. (2008). *The Key Poses of Yoga*. China: Banda Yoga
Publications, LLC.

Chapter 20

Foundation for Inner Peace, (2007). *A Course In Miracles,
Combined Volume.* Mill Valley, CA: Foundation for Inner
Peace
http://www.yogajournal.com/article/global/pranayama/
Long, R. (2008). *The Key Poses of Yoga*. China: Banda Yoga
Publications, LLC.

Chapter 21

https://www.brainyquote.com/quotes/authors/a/agnes_
de_mille.html

Chapter 22

Caplan, M, Axel, G. (2015). *Proceedings of the Yoga & Psyche
Conference (2014).* Newcastle upon Tyne: Cambridge
Scholars Publishing.

Felder, L. (2016). *More Fully Alive: The Benefits of Using Jewish Wisdom for Responding to Stress and Overload.* Los Angeles, CA: JFuture Books.

Hubbs, A. (2012). *Empower Yoga Teacher Training Manual,* Mantra Mind Body. New York, NY.

Chapter 23

Alcoholics Anonymous (1976). *Alcoholics Anonymous.* New York, NY: Alcoholics Anonymous World Services, Inc.

Alcoholics Anonymous (1952). *Twelve Steps and Twelve Traditions.* New York, NY: Alcoholics Anonymous World Services, Inc.

Williamson, M.(1975). *A Return To Love: Reflections on the Principles of A Course In Miracles.* Glen Ellen, CA: Foundation for Inner Peace.

Chapter 24

http://www.goodreads.com/quotes/424246-if-nothing-ever-changed-there-would-be-no-such-things

https://www.goodreads.com/work/quotes/12907434-the-candymakers (Wendy Mass quote).

https://www.amazon.com/Needs-Therapy-When-Have-Plaque/dp/B0013KUKW4

https://www.bustle.com/articles/166642-14-finding-nemo-quotes-to-remind-you-to-just-keep-swimming

Johnson, S. (2002). *Who Moved My Cheese?* New York, NY: Penguin Putnam Inc.

Levine, P. (2008). *Healing Trauma.* (p. 40). Boulder, CO: Sounds True, Inc.

Marlock, G, Weiss, H, Young, C, Soth, M. (2015). *The Handbook of Body Psychotherapy & Somatic Psychology.* Berkeley, CA: North Atlantic Books.

Chapter 25

Alcoholics Anonymous (1976). *Alcoholics Anonymous* 3rd Edition. (p. 449). New York, NY: Alcoholics Anonymous World Services, Inc.

Corsini, R. (2002). *The Dictionary of Psychology.* New York, NY: Brunner — Routledge.

Chapter 26

Andrews, T. (2009). *Animal-Speak Pocket Guide.* Jackson, TN: Dragonhawk Publishing.

Foundation for Inner Peace, (2007). *A Course In Miracles, Combined Volume.* Mill Valley, CA: Foundation for Inner Peace.

Long, R. (2008). *The Key Poses of Yoga.* China: Banda Yoga Publications, LLC.

Chapter 27

Allen, J. (1992). *The Five Stages of Getting Well.* Portland, OR: LifeTime Publishing.

Foundation for Inner Peace, (2007). *A Course In Miracles, Combined Volume.* Mill Valley, CA: Foundation for Inner Peace.

Turner, K. (2014). *Radical Remission: Surviving Cancer Against All Odds.* New York, NY: HarperCollins.

Chapter 28

Corey, G. (2001). Theory and Practice of Counseling and Psychotherapy. (p.100). Belmont, CA: Wadsworth/Thomson Learning.

Foundation for Inner Peace, (2007). *A Course In Miracles, Combined Volume.* Mill Valley, CA: Foundation for Inner Peace.

https://en.wikipedia.org/wiki/Ghost_(1990_film)

www.bookdesigner.com

Chapter 29

Eskenazi, T, Weiss, A. (2008). *The Torah, A Women's Commentary.* New York, NY: URJ Press.

Felder, L. (2016). *More Fully Alive: The Benefits of Using Jewish Wisdom for Responding to Stress and Overload.* Los Angeles, CA: JFuture Books.

http://www.chabad.org/library/article-cdo/aid/702209/jewish/Why -do-Jews-sway-while-praying.htm

https://en.wikipedia.org/wiki/Jewish_Renewal

http://www.jewfaq.org/shabbat.htm

https://en.wikipedia.org/wiki/Hindu_views_on_monotheism

Long, R. (2008). *The Key Poses of Yoga.* China: Banda Yoga Publications, LLC.

Chapter 30

Eskenazi, T, Weiss, A. (2008). *The Torah, A Women's Commentary.* New York, NY: URJ Press.
http://www.reiki-for-holistic-health.com/five-reiki-principles.html (reiki principles)

http://www.sacred-destinations.com/israel/jerusalem-west-
    ern-wall
https://en.wikipedia.org/wiki/Lord%27s_Prayer
Omartian, S. (2006). *A Book of Prayer, 365 Prayers for Victo-
    rious Living.* Eugene, OR: Harvest House Publishers.
www.katirussell.com
www.Reiki.org

Chapter 31

Adams, L, Strouse, C.(1960). *Put on a Happy Face*, from Bye
    Bye Birdie.
Ellison, K, P, Weingast, M. (2016-NY Zen Center for Contem-
    plative Care). *Awake at Bedside: Contemplative Teach-
    ings on Palliative and End-Of-Life Care.* Somerville, MA:
    Wisdom Publications.
Levine, P. (2008). *Healing Trauma.* (p.114). Boulder, CO:
    Sounds True, Inc.
Masters, R,A. (2010). *Spiritual Bypassing: When Spirituality
    Disconnects Us from What Really Matters.* Berkeley, CA:
    North Atlantic Books.
Turner, J, Parsons, G, Chaplan, C. (1936). *Smile* lyric and
    music.
Welwood, J. (2000). *Toward a Psychology of Awakening:
    Buddhism, Psychotherapy, and the Path of Personal and
    Spiritual Transformation.* Boston, MA: Shambhala Publi-
    cations, Inc.

Chapter 32

Tinkham, P. (2016). *Healing Trauma from the Inside Out*, Chapter 27, *A Course In Miracles* by David Asomaning, PhD. www.createspace.com.

Bibliography

Ajaya, S. (1983). *Psychotherapy East and West: a Unifying Paradigm.* Honesdale, PA: The Himalayan International Institute.

Alcoholics Anonymous (1952). *Twelve Steps and Twelve Traditions.* New York, NY: Alcoholics Anonymous World Services, Inc.

Allen, J. (1992). *The Five Stages of Getting Well.* Portland, OR: LifeTime Publishing.

American Psychiatric Association (2013). *Diagnostic and Statistical Manual of Mental Disorders, Fifth Edition, DSM 5- TM.* Washington, DC: American Psychiatric Association.

Andrews, T. (2009). *Animal-Speak Pocket Guide.* Jackson, TN: Dragonhawk Publishing.

Applied Sport Psychology (2007). *Psychological Benefits of Exercise,* www.appliedsportpsych.org/Resource-Center/health-and-fitness/articles/psych-benefits-of-exercise

Apsara Apothecary, Potions & Wyldcrafts by Tracy, wyldcrafter-aspara@yahoo.com

Atlantis, E, Chow CM, Kirby A, Singh MF (2004). An effective exercise based intervention for improving mental health and quality of life measures: a randomized controlled trial. *Journal of Preventive Medicine,* Aug, 39 (2): 424–34.

Banschick, M. (2011). *The Intelligent Divorce Because Your Kids Come First: Book Two: Taking Care of Yourself.* Stamford, CT: Intelligent Book Press.

Beck, A. (1976). *Cognitive Therapy And The Emotional Disorders.* New York, NY: Penguin Books.

Beck, J. (1995). *Cognitive Therapy: Basics and Beyond.* New York, NY: The Guilford Press.

Bently, K., Walsh, J.(2001). *The Social Worker and Psychotropic Medication: Second Edition: Toward Effective Collaboration with Mental Health Clients, Families, and Providers.* Belmont, California: Wadsworth.

Bernstein, E. (2016). *The Power of Feeling Down.* New York, NY: Wall Street Journal, Health and Wellness.

Berk, M. (2007). Intervention Insights: Should we be targeting exercise as a routine mental health intervention? *Acta Neuropsychiatrica, 19(3):* 217–218.

Berk, M. Felicity Ng, Seetal D. (2006). The effects of physical activity in the acute treatment of bipolar disorder: A pilot study. *Department of Clinical and Biomedical Sciences: Barwon Health,* University of Melbourne, Geelong, Victoria, Australia.

Berk, M., Felicity Ng, Seetal D., Felice N., Jacka, Leslie, E. (2007). Effects of a Walking Program in the Psychiatric In-patient Treatment Setting: A Cohort Study. *Health Promotional Journal of Australia, 18:39–42.*

Brosse, A. (2002). Exercise and the Treatment of Clinical Depression in Adults — Recent Findings and Future Directions. *Sports Medicine Journal, 32(12):* 741–760.

Campbell, J, Osbon, D. (1991). *Reflections on the Art of Living, A Joseph Campbell Companion.* New York, NY: HarperCollins Publishers.

Caplan, M, Axel, G. (2015). *Proceedings of the Yoga & Psyche Conference* (2014). Newcastle upon Tyne: Cambridge Scholars Publishing.

Caplan, M. (2011). *The Guru Question: The Perils and Rewards of Choosing a Spiritual Teacher.* Boulder, CO: Sounds True Inc.

Caplan, M. (2009). *Eyes Wide Open: Cultivating Discernment on the Spiritual Path.* Boulder, CO: Sounds True Inc.

Chopra, D. (1994). *The Seven Spiritual Laws of Success.* San Rafael, CA: Amber-Allen Publishing.

Choudhury, B. (2000). *Bikram's Beginning Yoga Class.* New York: Penguin Putnam.

Corsini, R. (2002). *The Dictionary of Psychology.* New York, NY: Brunner—Routledge.

Daley, A. (2002). Exercise Therapy and Mental Health in Clinical Populations: Is Exercise Therapy a Worldwide Intervention? *Advances in Psychiatric Treatment, 8:* 262–270, The Royal College of Psychiatrists.

Dyer, W. (2009). *Excuses Begone! How to Change Lifelong, Self-Defeating Thinking Habits.* New York, NY: Hay House Inc.

Emerson, D, Hopper, E (2011). *Overcoming Trauma through Yoga, Reclaiming your Body.* Berkeley, CA: North Atlantic Books.

Ellis, A. (2001). *New Directions for Rational Emotive Behavioral Therapy: Overcoming Destructive Beliefs, Feelings, and Behaviors.* New York, NY: Prometheus Books.

Ellison, K, P, Weingast, M. (2016—NY Zen Center for Contemplative Care). *Awake at Bedside: Contemplative Teachings on Palliative and End-Of-Life Care.* Somerville, MA: Wisdom Publications.

Eskenazi, T, Weiss, A. (2008). *The Torah, A Women's Commentary.* New York, NY: URJ Press.

Faulds, R. (2006). *Kripalu Yoga: A Guide to Practice On and Off the Mat.* New York: Bantam.

Faulds, D. (2006). *From Root to Bloom, Yoga Poems and Other Writings.* Kearney, NE: Morris Publishing.

Felder, L. (2016). *More Fully Alive: The Benefits of Using Jewish Wisdom for Responding to Stress and Overload.* Los Angeles, CA: JFuture Books.

Feuerstein, G. (1998). *Tantra: The Path of Ecstacy.* Boston, MA: Shambhala Publications, Inc.

Forbes, B. (2011). *Yoga For Emotional Balance: Simple Practices to Help Relieve Anxiety and Depression.* Boston, MA: Shambhala Publications, Inc.

Foundation for Inner Peace, (2007). *A Course In Miracles, Combined Volume.* Mill Valley, CA: Foundation for Inner Peace.

Gavin, G. (2006). A review of the latest research provides clues about what motivates people to exercise and what keeps them coming back. *Fitness Journal,* 39-45.

Germer, K., Siegel, R., Fulton, P. (2005). *Mindfulness and Psychotherapy.* New York: NY: The Guilford Press.

Geweniger-Bohlander (2014). *Pilates, A Teacher's Manual.* Heidelberg, Berlin: Springer Publishing.

Goleman, D. (1988). *The Meditative Mind: The Varieties of Meditative Experience.* New York, NY: Penguin Putnam, Inc.

Hanson, R. (2009). *Buddha's Brain: The Practical Neuroscience of Happiness, Love & Wisdom.* Oakland, CA: New Harbinger Publications Inc.

Hays, K. (1999). *Working it Out, Using Exercise in Psychotherapy.* Washington, DC: American Psychological Association.

Helliker, K (2005). Yet Another Reason to Go to the Gym: How Exercise Can Help Fight Depression. *Wall Street Journal,* May 10.

Herman, J. (1997). *Trauma and Recovery.* New York, NY: Basic Books.

Hirschi, G. (2000). *Mudras: Yoga in your Hands.* San Francisco, CA: Red Wheel/Weisler, LLC.

Howley, E., Franks, B., (1992). *Health Fitness Instructor's Handbook–2nd Edition.* Champaign, IL: Kinetics Books.

https://thebuddhistcentre.com/text/loving-kindness-meditation

http://www.chabad.org/library/article-cdo/aid/702209/jewish/Why -do-Jews-sway-while-praying.htm

http://jhyphen.tripod.com/history.html

http://www.yogajournal.com/article/beginners/the-eight-limbs/

Hubbs, A. (2012). *Empower Yoga Teacher Training Manual,* Mantra Mind Body. New York, NY.

Hyman, M. (2009). *The UltraMind Solution: The Simple Way to Defeat Depression, Overcome Anxiety, and Sharpen Your Mind.* New York, NY: Simon & Schuster, Inc.

Johnsgard, K. (2004). *Conquering Depression & Anxiety Through Exercise.* Amherst, NY: Prometheus Books.

Johnson, S. (2002). *Who Moved My Cheese?* New York, NY: Penguin Putnam Inc.

Joseph, T, Fallo-Mitchell, L. (2014). *Everyday Mystic: Finding the Extraordinary in the Ordinary.*

Kabat-Zinn, J. (1994). *Wherever You Go There You Are: Mindfulness Meditation in Everyday Life.* New York, NY: Hachette Books.

Kabat-Zinn, J, Segal, Z, Teasdale, J, Williams, M. (2007). *The Mindful Way through Depression: Freeing Yourself from Chronic Unhappiness.* New York, NY: The Guilford Press.

Karp, H. (2006). Working Out Your Anxiety, *Wall Street Journal, August 6.*

Kaufman, M. (2007) Albert Ellis, Provoker of Change in Psychotherapy, Is Dead at 93. *The New York Times,* July 25.

Kirschenbaum, D. (2005). *The Healthy Obsession Program: Smart Weight Loss Instead of Low-Carb Lunacy.* Dallas, TX: BenBella Books, Inc.

Langreth, R. (2007) Patient Fix Thyself, *Forbes,* April 9.

Lasater, J. (2000). *Living Your Yoga.* Berkley, CA: Rodmell Press.

Lee,C. (2004). *Yoga Body, Buddha Mind.* New York, NY: Riverhead Books.

Levine, P. (2015). *Trauma and Memory: Brain and Body in A Search For The Living Past, A Practical Guide for Understanding and Working with Traumatic Memory.* Berkeley, CA: North Atlantic Books.

Levine, P. (1997). *Waking the Tiger: Healing Trauma.* Berkeley, CA: North Atlantic Books.

Levine, P. (2010). *In An Unspoken Voice: How the Body Releases Trauma and Restores Goodness.* Berkeley, CA: North Atlantic Books.

Linehan, M. (1993). *Skills Training Manual for Treating Borderline Personality Disorder.* New York, NY: Guilfore Publications, Inc.

Mann, D. (2010). *Gestalt Therapy: 100 Key Points & Techniques.* New York, NY: Routledge.

Marlock, G, Weiss, H, Young, C, Soth, M. (2015). *The Handbook of Body Psychotherapy & Somatic Psychology.* Berkeley, CA: North Atlantic Books.

Masters, R,A. (2010). *Spiritual Bypassing: When Spirituality Disconnects Us from What Really Matters.* Berkeley, CA: North Atlantic Books.

Miller, M. (2005). Working Off Depression. *Harvard Mental Health Letter,* December issue.

Miller, M. (2003). Questions and Answers. *Harvard Mental Health Letter,* June issue.

Nagourney, E. (2005). Mental Health: Sweating Depression Away. *New York Times,* Feb. 1.

NurrieStearns, M. (2010). *Yoga for Anxiety: Meditations and Practices for Calming The Body and Mind.* Oakland, CA: Raincoast Books.

Office of the Surgeon General, US Department of Health and Human Services (2007). *Overweight and Obesity: What You Can Do.*

Omartian, S. (2006). *A Book of Prayer, 365 Prayers for Victorious Living.* Eugene, OR: Harvest House Publishers.

Peeke, P. (2007). Integrative fitness, The New Science of Body-Mind Medicine. *IDEA Fitness Journal,* June Issue.

Peschek-Bohmer, F, Schreiber, G. (2002). *Healing Crystals and Gemstones: From Amethyst to Zircon, A comprehensive listing of the therapeutic uses and healing effects of the most important crystals and gemstones.* Old Saybrook, CT: Konecky & Konecky.

Picard, A. (2006). Jog Your Way to a Healthier Heart and Brain: What keeps your heart strong may also keep your mind sharp, researchers suggest. *Toronto Globe and Mail,* Feb. issue.

Pond, D. (1999). *Chakras For Beginners: A guide to Balancing Your Chakra Energies.* Woodbury, MN: Llewellyn Publications.

Rama, S. (1976). *Yoga and Psychotherapy: The Evolution of Consciousness.* Honesdale, PA: The Himalayan International Institute.

Rand, W. (1991). *Reiki The Healing Touch: First and Second Degree Manual.* Southfield, MI: Vision Publications.

www.Reiki.org

Richardson, C., Faulkner, G., McDevitt, J., Skrinar, G., Hutchinson, D., Piette, J. (2005). Integrating Physical Activity Into Mental Health Services for Persons With Serious Mental Illness. *Psychiatric Services,* March, 56(3): 324-331.

Saleebey, D. (2002). *The Strengths Perspective in Social Work Practice, 3rd Edition.* Boston, MA: Pierson Education Company.

Satchidananda, S. (2011). *The Yoga Sutras of Patanjali.* Buckingham, VA: Satchidananda Ashram, Integral Yoga Publications.

Satchidananda, S. (1988). *The Living Gita: the Complete Bhagavad Gita.* Buckingham, VA: Satchidananda Ashram — Yogaville, Inc.

Seligman, M. (2002). *Authentic Happiness: Using the New Positive Psychology to Realize Your Potential for Lasting Fulfillment.* New York, NY: Free Press.

Servan-Schreiber,D. (2004). Run For Your Life. *Psychotherapy Networker,* July/August issue.

Siegel, R, Germer, C, Fulton, P. (2005). Mindfulness and Psychotherapy. New York, NY: The Guilford Press.

Smits, J., Otto, M. (2009). *Exercise for Mood and Anxiety Disorders: Therapist Guide: Treatments That Work.* New York, NY: Oxford University Press.

Thurman, H. (1976). Jesus and the Disinherited. Boston, Massachusetts: Beacon Press Books.

Tinkham, P. (2008). *Stamford Plus Magazine, Soulmates, The psychological relationship between us and our pets and how they can keep us sane,* Fall, 2008, Stamfordplus.com.

Tinkham, P. (2010). *Reiki I—Teaching Manual.* Stamford, CT.

Turner, K. (2014). *Radical Remission: Surviving Cancer Against All Odds.* New York, NY: HarperCollins.

USABP, (2016). *United States Association for Body Psychotherapy, The Hub of Somatic Psychology,* http://usabp.org/.

Van Der Kolk, B. (2014). *The Body Keeps the Score: Brain, Mind, and Body in the Healing of Trauma.* New York, NY: Penguin Books.

Virtue, D. (1998). *Chakra Clearing: Awakening Your Spiritual Power to Know and Heal.* Carlsbad, CA: Hay House Inc.

Weintraub, A. (2004). *Yoga for Depression: A Compassionate Guide to Relieve Suffering Through Yoga.* New York, NY: Broadway Books.

Weintraub, A. (2012). *Yoga Skills for Therapists: Effective Practices for Mood Management.* New York, NY: W.W.Norton & Company.

Welwood, J. (2000). *Toward a Psychology of Awakening: Buddhism, Psychotherapy, and the Path of Personal and Spiritual Transformation.* Boston, MA: Shambhala Publications, Inc.

Williams & Wilkins (1995). *ACSM Guidelines for Exercise Testing and Prescription, Fifth Edition.* Media, PA: American College of Sports Medicine.

Williams, M., Teasdale, J., Segal, Z., Kabat-Zinn, J. (2007). *The Mindful Way through Depression: Freeing Yourself From Chronic Unhappiness.* New York, NY: The Guilford Press.

Williamson, M.(1975). *A Return To Love: Reflections on the Principles of A Course In Miracles.* Glen Ellen, CA: Foundation for Inner Peace.

www.ouramazingworld.org/spirituality/the-7-chakras-the-basics-explored-for-beginners

www.katirussell.com

www.Reiki.org

Yalom, I. (1980). *Existential Psychotherapy.* New York, NY: Basic Books.

Index

Made in the USA
Middletown, DE
22 February 2023